Testing the Angels

Floyd DeBurger

DISCLAIMER

This book is a memoir. It reflects my present memories of experiences over time. Some names and characteristics have been changed, some events have been condensed, and some conversation has been reconstructed.

Email: fdeburger@gmail.com

© 2017 by Floyd DeBurger
All rights reserved
Printed in the United States of America

ISBN 9781545234365

DEDICATION

I dedicate this book to my Grandpa, Grandma & Uncle George. My life would be nothing today without their positive influence on my life. I will always love them and look forward to seeing them again in Heaven.

THANK YOU TO MY WIFE, JUDY

my earthly angel

INTRODUCTION

It is 3 am in the morning and I am awakened by a slight noise and light coming from the living area. I am usually a very heavy sleeper unlike my husband Floyd who has suffered from insomnia ever since his triple bypass heart surgery in 1995. He regularly gets up in the middle of the night so to me nothing is unusual on this night except that I can't go back to sleep. So I decide to get up and visit with Floyd. As I sleepily walk into the living room I see Floyd sitting at the desk writing in a spiral notebook. I casually ask him what he is doing as I assume he is probably working on the budget as we are always on a tight budget and he is quite the number cruncher. He looks at me funny and doesn't say a word as he hands me a spiral notebook.

I am puzzled as I look at his scribbled words on the pages. His handwriting is so horrid, it is barely legible. I flip through the pages and notice he has handwritten over 60 pages! I ask him what he is writing about. He says nothing, but looks at me like a pitiful child and starts crying. This alarms me because I have never seen Floyd cry even at his Mother's funeral. He is always so stoic and strong. So I sit down and get out my reading glasses and proceed to read about Floyd's life.

I am so surprised he has written so much about his life as he has never written any letters or even hardly a sentence in any card. He once told me he never even wrote a paragraph for any teacher during his school years. In various jobs he used a Dictaphone or carried a small tape recorder so his secretary could take care of all of his correspondence. He did this to hide his dyslexia (which he discovered later in life) and poor writing skills. As I muddled through his poor handwriting, spelling, and grammar I am captivated by his straightforward words about his life.

As I read, I learn things I never knew about Floyd even though we have been married for 14 years. It shocks me to learn of his physical and mental abuse he suffered at the hands of his step-father. Floyd always talked about how much he loved his mother and what a good mother she was to him. However as I read his life story I sense he feels great abandonment and neglect from his mother throughout his childhood.

Over the next 18 years I continued to help Floyd with his memoir by trying to transcribe his story as best I could, which was not easy due to his appalling handwriting and lack of punctuation use. I even had some copy editing work done on his book but I had to be very careful not to lose his voice in the telling of his growing up years. So yes there are places where he uses improper pronouns or verbs, but this is needed to keep his voice authentic and alive as he tells his life story.

I am a retired school librarian and continually find myself amazed at how he felt so compelled to write about his life. We all have a story to tell but few find the motivation to tell it, especially in written form. I am very proud of my husband for having the courage and undaunted determination to share his life in this book. I have learned more about my husband and his inner soul by reading his heartbreaking story of neglect and poverty. It is my wish that his memoir not only helps his children and their children after them to understand family events from their past, but to also help others release their hidden pains and sorrows of childhood. Even to this day, Floyd cannot talk about the events in this book without crying as the child in him is still healing.

Judy DeBurger

Floyd (age 5) with dog Penny

1937, My Family's Great Depression

I was born on March 4, 1938, in Phoenix, Arizona, where my parents had moved six months earlier. I remember my mother telling me how poor we were. We lived in a little two-room house when I was born and I had two older sisters and an older brother. I remember later Mother talking about how small the rooms were. We had no beds, my parents had a mattress but we kids just made pallets on the floor. The house was so small there was no room to walk when all the pallets were made up.

I never really knew if my father drank a lot or if he was just lazy and had no ambition. I just know how Mother talked about him being gone for two or three days at a time and he'd say he was working but he never brought any money home. When I was a few months old we got kicked out of our house and all of our things were moved out of the house into the road.

My dad came home when he heard about this and he borrowed a wagon and a team of mules. We loaded all the things up, which wasn't very much, just a small dining table and two chairs, very little clothes, and a few dishes along with a couple of pots and pans.

Mother said Dad told her he knew a place we could stay that was better because it wouldn't cost any money. This place was a hole in the side of the mountain. Mother sometimes called it a dugout and other times a cave. She didn't know just how far it was from town, but it took most of the day for us to get there.

My two sisters were old enough to walk alongside the wagon and kick rocks and play a little. I was only three months old and my brother was about two years old. So my mother had her hands full taking care of us children.

We finally could see the side of the mountain and a hole in it and my dad pointed and said this is where we would stay for a few days. We got to the bottom of the mountain and there was a narrow walkway up to the hole's opening. My mother and dad had to carry their mattress and our few belongings up the walk. Mother almost fell off the path a couple of times, the slope of the walk was so steep, it was almost straight down, and if she would have fallen, it would have been about a thirty to forty foot drop.

Once we got unloaded, they laid the mattress on the ground in the cave and Mother put me and my brother on it and we slept while she fixed us something to eat. The next day we didn't have much to eat so Mother went down the dirt road to a little church we had passed the day before. They gave her enough food to last for a few days. By that time my dad had got a job working on a farm and we were able to buy food. We had everything we really needed living in the cave and we had no rent or utilities to pay.

Mother later said things got better between her and Dad for a while. We had plenty to eat and she thought it was much cooler living in the cave. Since this was in the middle of the summer in Arizona, the temperature had to be over a hundred degrees and I guess in the cave it was probably five to ten degrees cooler. As the summer went on, my two sisters and brother played in a little creek that ran along the bottom edge of the mountainside and it had a few places where it was ten to twelve feet wide and about two feet deep. It made a good place for them to cool off. It would give my mother a little time to relax and hold and feed me. She would sit in a chair at the front of the cave and watch them play. This also made a good place for her to wash clothes. The creek was spring-fed and the water was very clear where it was running over the rocks. This was also our drinking water.

Well, the summer passed and the cooler weather began to start. Being on the south side of the mountain, the sun would shine in and keep us very warm and we never got any of the cold north wind. Mother enjoyed sitting in the front of the cave in the sun even when it was very cold outside. When winter came, work for my dad was slow so Mother had to start going back to the little country church and ask for food.

Everything began to go very bad as my brother got sick and we had no money to take him to a doctor. Mother tried to be a good Christian and attended the little church down the road. When Kenneth got sick, the only thing she knew to do was take him to the church which believed in faith healing and asks the church people to pray for him. As time went on, he got sicker and sicker and my dad started staying gone for three or four days at a time. Mother said the stress of taking care of us children and not having enough food along with my brother being sick was almost more than she could bear.

Well, Kenneth continued to be sick and that winter he died at the age of two. Mother said she thought he died of pneumonia or whooping cough. I was only about nine months old when he passed away. How mother got through this I don't know. If that happened to me when my children were little, I'm not sure how I would have gone on living. Just the thought of one of my children dying at the age of two is almost more than I can bear to think about. To this day, I don't know where my brother Kenneth is buried as I never asked my Mother because I was afraid it would upset her.

I think my mother's love for us kids and her being very strong-willed is what got her through this difficult time. After my brother died, my dad just disappeared, leaving us stranded way out there on the side of that mountain.

Oklahoma Bound

After a couple of weeks, someone from the little church down the road told Mother about a couple planning a trip to Oklahoma and they said we could ride with them. My mother was from Oklahoma and her mother and dad still lived out in the country on a farm. The closest town to them was Foster, Oklahoma and the next town over was Elmore City. Mother said she thought God made it possible for us to get a ride back home. The people we rode with had a Model A Ford and the back seat was not very big. But that is where Mother, I and my two sisters rode while the couple taking us along rode up front. Mother said it took about four days to get to Oklahoma because the roads were so bad and it rained most of the way. There were a lot of the roads that weren't paved, so we had to stop a lot because of the mud on the road. One night the rain and mud was so bad we had to sleep in the car. Another night the couple paid for us to stay in a motel, plus they fed us all the way home.

Mother said she had never stayed in a motel before and eating all that good food at the restaurants made her feel like we were on a vacation. Well, I never saw my dad again until I was fourteen years old (My thoughts about him certainly didn't improve with that meeting and that's all I need say about that). Mother tried to find him to get child support for us kids, but no luck. My dad's parents lived close to Oklahoma City and I was later told they had plenty of money but refused to help us at all. They knew where my dad was, but would not tell Mother, so she had to support all of us children by herself.

My mother's parents were very poor, they lived on a little forty-acre farm that my Grandpa and Grandma were sharecropping along with my mother's brother, Uncle George. They only had a team of mules and some farm equipment like a plow, a harrow, a disc, and a planter. All of these were pulled by a team of mules. My Uncle George had to walk behind the plow and guide the different farm parts along. This team of mules was also used to pull a wagon to town for us to get supplies. Most of the time we only went to Foster about once a month, but sometimes we would go all the way to Elmore City. This was a little town that was only about four blocks long and had no paved streets, all were just dirt. I don't think they even had any gravel back then, but even with just the dirt roads and only four blocks long, it was called Elmore City.

Mother didn't talk much about what happened after we came back to Grandmother and Grandpa's farm. All I know is that she and my two sisters only stayed there a few months until Mother got a job in Elmore City as a housekeeper and caretaker. She and my sisters moved to Elmore City and I stayed with Grandma, Grandpa, and Uncle George.

My Uncle George was about thirty years old at this time and had never married. In fact, he never got married until both Grandma and Grandpa had passed away. He was about sixty when Grandma passed away and surprised us all by getting married just a few months later. When we first came back from Arizona, my Grandpa was 67 years old and unable to do much on the farming, so my Uncle George did most of the heavy work. And when needed, my grandmother worked on the farm with my uncle.

Life on the "Mountain"

I was too young to remember much that went on while we lived on the little farm north of Foster. I do remember one time we went to town and the town people asked where we lived, Uncle George would tell them we lived on the mountain and everybody would know where we lived. They would respond, 'Yep, ya'll live up thar by so-an'-so,' and Uncle George would say 'Yep, jest a mile o' two down th' road.' I have driven back there several times since I have been grown and I look around and only see a very large hill. It still puzzles me how the town people always knew where we lived just by us saying, "the mountain". I don't know why but this really sticks in my mind.

When we went to town it would be an all-day affair. My Uncle George would get up about daybreak and start hitching up the mules to the wagon. He would first make sure the mules were fed real good before he put on their harnesses and hooked them up to the wagon. Going to town was very exciting for me because we only went about once a month. We would go all the way to Elmore City and I would get to see my mother. When I think back and put the dates of when this happened, I figure I was about three or four years old. One thing I really liked to do as we were going to town was to jump off the wagon and run as fast as I could while grabbing hold of the wagon and running along behind it. As long as I didn't lose my footing, I could go a long way. Sometimes the wagon was pulling me along faster than I could run and I would lose my footing as my feet went straight out behind me. My knees would be dragging the ground and Grandma would yell to Uncle George to stop the wagon. When the wagon stopped, Grandma would help me into the wagon and my knees would be all skinned up.

For some reason, we always carried a can of kerosene with us and anytime I had a cut or a scrape, Grandma would put some kerosene on it. I don't know what the medical profession would think of that today, but I think she knew something they didn't. Because I don't remember ever getting an infection from cuts or scrapes as the kerosene helped heal me up really fast.

One time when I was about six years old, I was climbing through on some old boards with nails sticking up everywhere. I tripped and fell and one of those nails went into the palm of my hand and was sticking out the back side of my hand. The nail was still stuck to a board and now my hand was stuck to the board. I picked up the board with my left hand, holding it tight against the palm of my right hand and ran for the house. My Grandma was sitting on the front porch and heard me crying. She came running, picked me up and set me on the porch and told me to hold the board tight against me with my left hand and she would be right back.

She came back with a pan filled with enough kerosene to cover my hand. Then she reached over and took hold of the board with one hand and my right hand with the other. She looked at me and I looked at her and I knew what she was going to do next! So I braced myself and got ready because I knew there was no other way. She gave a big jerk and the nail came out. By then I think my body decided it didn't need to register any more pain because it didn't seem to hurt at all. Grandma took my hand and put it in the pan of kerosene and told me to keep it completely submerged for at least thirty minutes. That evening before I went to bed, I soaked my hand in a pan of kerosene and Grandma wrapped it with a clean white rag. The next morning I did the same thing again and in a couple of days, I was playing like nothing had happened.

That board with the nail in it had to be laying there for a long time because the nail was so rusty that the palm of my hand had rust all on it and in it. To this day, I don't know if it was the kerosene that healed all my scrapes or if my Grandma had used an old Indian healing herb or if my guardian angels were looking over me. All I know is that Grandma's remedies seemed to work miracles on my body and it is a good thing because I was very accident-prone and needed one of those miracles about once a week.

Time to See Mother

The first time I remember going to town, it seemed like we would never get there. It seemed like hours to me back then, but when I go back there and drive down the old dirt road (by the way, it is still a dirt road) up on the mountain it only takes a short time. I guess back then it took the mules and wagon about an hour to get to Foster and another forty-five minutes to Elmore City.

Well, we finally got to Elmore City. As we came into town, there was a creek with a little wooden bridge across it only wide enough for one wagon. I remember being a little bit scared that the bridge would fall in but would thank God after we made it. We went back to town several times, and after crossing the same little bridge with it never falling down, I finally decided that bridges were okay. After we crossed the bridge, we came to another street where we had to turn left. That was Main Street of what I thought at the time was a very big city, "Elmore City!" The population in 1940 was 494 and the population today is around 725.

Main Street was about two blocks long, with stores on both sides of the street. I remember a hardware store, drug store, feed store, post office and grocery store. There were several other stores but these are the ones I remember well. As we came down Main that day, the street was almost knee deep in mud (at least my 4 year old knees) because of the rain the day before. All the horses and wagons going down Main

Street made it one big mud hole. We parked the wagon and mules at the end of town in a lot where a bunch of other wagons were parked. Uncle George got out, took a bucket of feed and put it in front of the mules so they could eat, and we started walking down Main Street. We walked on the wooden walkways as much as we could, but there were some places we had to walk in the mud and, my being a little boy, I would step in the mud every chance I got and Grandma would say, "Git out of that thar mud, ya hafta wear them clothes all day long an' I don't wancha t' be all wet an' muddy 'cause ya will ketch a death of cold on th' way home in th' cool night air."

Grandma and Uncle George went on their way to shop for all our needs while me and my Grandpa sat on an old wooden bench in front of the feed store. Everybody that came by seemed to know my Grandpa and would stop and talk for several minutes. And they would all tease me and say I was too little to be coming into town, that coming to town was a man's thing and they would say, "Do ya have any money?" and I would say no and they would say, "If ya don't have any money, how comes ya come t' town?" and Grandpa and them would laugh. And after they were gone, Grandpa would say, "They don't knows I don't have any money either," and we would laugh.

Grandpa lost his eye when he was thirty-two years old. He told me he was chopping wood with an axe and a wood chip flew up and hit him in the eye. They were so poor that he didn't go to the doctor until it was infected. The doctor had to take his eye out. Since he was too poor to get a glass eye, Grandpa just had a sunk-in place where his eyeball used to be. My cousins and I never thought much about it, since that was the way Grandpa looked all our life.

By this time, it was about dinnertime (back then, we called lunch dinnertime and the evening meal supper). Uncle George and Grandma came back and we headed back to the wagon to eat. Grandma had made a pot of beans and cornbread and a few biscuits. The biscuits were for me, I liked biscuits with peanut butter and jelly on it.

All the food had to be kept cold. Grandma had this big pail of water and a smaller pail that set down in it and all the food that needed to be kept cool and dry would be in the small pail and it would set in the water in the bigger pail. We also had a jug of milk, what we'd probably call a half-gallon carton today. Only the jug was a half gallon glass bottle.

We would climb up in the wagon, Grandma, Grandpa, and Uncle George would get a bowl of beans & cornbread and a cup of milk. By this time, the beans, cornbread, and milk were all the same temperature, which was just a bit cool. Grandma would fix me two or three biscuits with peanut butter and jelly on them, a small cup of beans with a little cornbread and a cup of milk. By the way, a cup was not a coffee cup as we know today; these were more like a twelve or fourteen-ounce cups, except these cups were made of tin metal, so in today's world, about the same size as a tall glass of milk.

As soon as we finished eating, Uncle George said we could go see my mother. I don't know why we had to wait till after we ate to go see her. Maybe Grandma and Uncle George needed to get their supplies bought first or they didn't want to disturb her while she was working. Anyway, we waited until after dinner to head over to see her.

I had not seen where my mother and sisters were living or where Mother was working, so I was pretty excited about seeing all this. We walked because it was only one street over from Main Street and about two or three blocks down that street, so it only took us a few minutes to get there. It would not have taken so long if it had not been so wet and muddy and Grandma not wanting me to get wet and muddy. But sometimes I think Grandpa didn't care, because when he held my hand, he would just head for the mud puddles. Grandma would say, "Daddy," —that is what she always called Grandpa—"Daddy, don't let 'im step in that thar mud hole." And Grandpa would look at me and kind of snicker under his breath and I would laugh. Grandma would say, "Let me hold his hand', 'cause ya can't' keep him outta that mud."

When we got to the house where my mother was working—it was a huge two-story house—I just stood there looking at it like it was the tallest building in the world. It was the first two-story house I had ever seen. I was standing there staring for so long that Grandma finally said, "Whut's wrong? Come on, let's see yer mom." Uncle George reached down and picked me up and we started toward a little house in back of the huge one.

I heard my mother's voice calling from the back of the big house where she worked, "I'm in here, I'll be out in just a minute." The sound of her voice almost made me start crying. I bit my lip and held the tears in because I didn't want to make her sad. I felt like I did back on the mountain when I overheard my Grandma and Uncle George talking about how hard it was for my mother to leave me with them.

Grandma said, "Poor Gladys, she makes barely enough money t'support herself an' th' girls, I think she should leave little Pumpkin with us fer a spell longer."

It seemed everyone thought it best for me to stay on the farm. Mother said, "I love you, sweetie, but the best thing for you is to stay here with Grandma, Grandpa and Uncle George. I promise you, when you get older you can come live with me. I'll never let our family down like this again!" I can still feel the hurt inside of being left behind by my mother during that time of my life.

I loved her so much and I would fantasize about what a beautiful and wonderful mother I had, only she couldn't make enough money to let me live with her. She was pretty, about 5'2" with a petite body and long dark wavy hair. When we went to see her that day in Elmore City, she was in her late twenties. Now that I am grown, the earliest picture I have of my mother is at age thirty-five. But in my mind's eye, I can still see how pretty she looked to me on that day.

She was book smart too, at least when she was in grade school, she would always win the spelling bee at school and do better than anyone in her class in math. However, she never went past the eighth grade which did not help her in finding good jobs. It was very uncommon in the early 1940s for a woman to be single and supporting three children.

Well, I held back my crying and ran to her grabbing her around the neck, giving her a big hug. She must have told me five times how much she missed me and she loved me. This was probably not the first time we came to town to see her, but it is the first time I remember. The little house she lived in was very small. My sisters came home from school and we played for what seemed a little while and then it was time to leave. We had to leave because it would take a couple of hours to get home on the wagon and we had to get home before dark.

As we waved good-bye to my mother and sisters, I almost started crying again but held it back because I didn't want her to see me cry. We walked back to Main Street and Grandpa and Uncle George got the wagon and brought it to load up the feed for the animals and everything else they'd bought at the feed store. While they took care of loading, Grandma and I went inside and picked out some flour sacks. She always made my shirts from flour sacks and would let me go with her to pick out from the many different printed patterns on the sacks.

I don't remember riding home…..I guess I fell asleep on the hand-quilted blanket Grandma always brought along because it had been a long, exciting day for a four-year-old boy.

My mother, Gladys, always had a hard life. Partly due to her choices and stubborn will. She could have lived with my Uncle George and her parents, but she chose to strike out in life alone. She always worked for low wages and many times would work two jobs just to have enough money for us to survive. Even though she was somewhat "book smart," when I look back at some of her decisions, I don't think she had a lot of common sense. She thought what she was doing was best for the family. She would try different things and different jobs but was never able to use her intelligence to make a better life for herself or her children. But she was a giving person and spent what little money she had on us children and never on herself.

I don't really know how my mother and dad got together. It turned out to be one of the worst things of her life. I was told by relatives that when she was young, she was high-spirited and rebellious and wanted to do things her way. Getting married young was a way to get away from her parents. Throughout life, I noticed that she was impulsive and made quick decisions without thinking about the consequences. Her bad marriage to my dad caused her to not trust men for a long time. I wondered why she couldn't find a nice man like my Uncle George, who seemed to make good decisions all the time. But when she did trust a man again, she thought she had found the dream of her life.

She was always sweet and kind, at least towards me. Her sister, my Aunt Ruth, used to tell me that Mom made the best grades in school but was stubborn and lacked common sense, so she never lasted long on her jobs.

Uncle George and the Model T

One of the main memories I have of living with Uncle George was when he bought a Model T Ford. Shortly after he bought it, we took a trip to Pauls Valley, Oklahoma, to buy Grandma a new Singer pedal sewing machine. The car's trunk was a big box mounted on the back of the car; it was built like an old trunk that people would put at the foot of their bed. Whenever I hear someone talking about the trunk of their care, I visualize Uncle George's old Model T.

He couldn't get the sewing machine all the way in the trunk, so he had to leave the trunk lid open and tie the sewing machine down. On the way home, it began to rain and the dirt roads got muddy. Every time we started up a hill, we would start to slip and slide until we got stuck. Uncle George would get out and start pushing while Grandpa steered. We made it almost all the way home when we came to the road at the foot of the mountain that led to our farm. It was steep and about a quarter of a mile long. Uncle George pushed with Grandpa driving but we didn't make any headway. So Grandma got out to help push and the car started to slowly move up the hill.

Whenever the car took off going up the hill, Uncle George and Grandma would jump on the back bumper and ride until it got stuck again. Everything was going pretty good until the car slowed down in the deep mud and began to slide off the right side of the road into a bar ditch. It was raining even harder and we were all soaked to the bone. We all knew this was as far as the car was going for now. We had to leave the car and Grandma's new sewing machine sitting in the rain. Poor Grandma thought her new sewing machine was a goner, but Uncle George assured her he could fix it and it would be like new again.

We got what we could carry out of the car and started walking in the rain up the muddy road. Uncle George carried me most of the way. When we reached the top of the mountain, he put me down and I had to walk another half a mile down the dirt road to the farmhouse. We got home and dried ourselves off sitting by the old potbellied stove.

Uncle George and Grandpa had to wait a couple of days for the rain to stop then they hitched up a team of mules and took a chain to hook the car onto the mules' harness. When we got to the car, they looked over everything that had got wet and some parts of the sewing machine had started to rust. Uncle George said, "It'll clean up with a little oiling'." We hooked the car bumper to the wagon, Uncle George took the reins and Grandpa got in the driver's seat to guide the car. I sat on the front seat beside him and gave Uncle George the signal for the mules to start pulling and they pulled that old Model T right out of the ditch.

After we got the car up on the road, Uncle George tried to start it again but the motor wouldn't go. We got ready to pull the car home when Grandpa said, "Pumpkin, git behind' this here wheel an' drive this here car home fer us." He looked at Uncle George when he said this and Uncle George just nodded and said, "Are ya shure he's old enough t'drive?" Grandpa said, "Yep, an' when we git home, I'm going to learn him t' drive these mules so he can do all th' plowing'." My first experience at driving: a four-year-old steering the wheel of a Model T while a team of mules pulled it. I thought I was mighty big and doing big man driving! It took us most of the day to get the car home but I got to steer it all the way. We got home shortly before dark and were covered with mud from head to toe.

Grandma had fixed us a big pot of pinto beans with cornbread and homemade butter. I don't even remember if Uncle George ever got that car to run again. I do remember that was the summer my mother, sisters, and all my cousins came to visit.

Playing House
While they were visiting, a couple of neighbor girls that lived a mile down the road came over to play with my cousins and sisters after dinner. All the grown-ups were sitting on the porch talking and dipping stuff. All of us kids went down to the barn to play. We liked to play house in an old covered wagon in the barn. I was the youngest and also the only boy. There were seven girls (my two sisters, three cousins, and two neighbor girls) all between ten to twelve years old.

When we played house, I always played the part of the "baby boy" of the family. We were playing regular house for a while with girls making mud pies. I was the little boy that was getting into everything and acting rowdy. Then one of the girls decided it was time to change my diaper (pretending I was a baby). But I wasn't going for this because I really wasn't a baby and my pants didn't need changing. I decided to go along with them. They laid me on the bench inside the covered wagon and one of the girls began to unbutton my pants and pull them down. By then all the girls were laughing and giggling. Now I lay there with my bottom hanging out and I was so embarrassed. Lucky for me, just then Grandma called, "Time t' eat ... supper is ready...y'all kids come on in now."

At that time I was around four years old and Mother had taken a job in Oklahoma City working for the Wilson Meat Packing Plant. I didn't get to see her much since she didn't live in Elmore City anymore. So when she moved to Oklahoma City, in my little child's mind, I didn't think I would ever see her again. When she came to say goodbye, I had a real hard time hugging her. I was afraid I would cry and, at the same time, I was mad at her for taking a job farther away from me. I felt I had to be strong and not cry, so I gave her a big hug and ran off to take my dog for a long walk over the edge of the mountain. I wasn't even back at the house in time to wave bye to my mother when she drove off.

Drugstore 'Cowboy'

One very hot day that summer, my Grandparents, Uncle George, and I went to Elmore City. Uncle George took me by the hand and said, "Come on Pumpkin—go with me. Grandma, you an' Pa wait here. Pumpkin an' I'll be back in a minute."

We went walking down the old wooden sidewalk for about a block. Finally, I asked, "Uncle George, where are we going?"

"Jest ya wait, Pumpkin, ya'll see when we git t' th' drugstore."

When we walked in the door, there was a long bar on the right that went all the way to the back of the store. There were barstools on the customer side and shiny soda bar equipment on the other side. I had never been in here before and I just stood amazed. I could barely see the soda jerk man behind the bar because it was so tall. Uncle George picked me up and set me on a barstool. I could see everything in the soda fountain now. There was shiny chrome everywhere. I had never seen chrome before and I was in awe with its shininess. It looked almost like a mirror.

There was a big black grill with burgers cooking and they smelled wonderful. All the soda glasses were hanging on the wall. I had never seen so many different shapes and sizes of glasses. Some had big long stems, which I thought must have been just for looks because if you put anything in them they looked like they would fall over. All the sudden, I realized Uncle George had been trying to get my attention. I must have been sitting in a daze for several minutes.

When I finally answered him, he and the drugstore soda jerk laughed at me. The soda jerk said, "I don't think I've seen ya in here before." I didn't even answer him because I was still gazing around like I was in some kind of fairy tale. Uncle George said, "Give this little fella an ice cream cone."

The soda jerk pulled a cone out from a big, tall chrome thing sticking up from the counter and asked, "Chocolate or vanilla?" As he looked at me for an answer, I just kept looking around at all the things in the store like I was in shock. Uncle George answered for me, "Make it vanilla."

Glued to my barstool, I watch the soda jerk take a big silver ice cream dipper and open a big container of ice cream and start dipping. He put two big dips on a cone. I just sat there, watching and wondering where all this ice cream comes from. The soda jerk handed me the ice cream and told Uncle George, "That'll be five cents."

As Uncle George reached into his pocket for the money, I started to lick the ice cream and the soda jerk gruffly said, "Don't you lick that until it's paid for." Uncle George gave him the money and we left. I was afraid to lick on the ice cream until we were out of the soda jerk's sight. I never knew if he was joking or not and wonder if he meant it because we looked so poor.

Tornado Ready?

After my Mother moved to Oklahoma City, Uncle George found a forty-acre farm north of Elmore City to sharecrop. It was better farmland and the owner offered him a larger share of the money from the crops. The farmhouse was nicer than the one on the mountain. It had one major problem: there wasn't a storm cellar. Grandma *had* to have a storm cellar. "I ain't movin' t' th' new farm unless ya promise t' build me a cellar."

Uncle George's first project was to dig that storm cellar. He dug a hole in the ground that was deep enough for a person to stand up and wide enough for five to six people. It was about eight feet wide and twelve feet long. He used a pick and shovel to dig the hole. Every day after the farm chores were done, he would work on the hole, so it took him almost two months to finish the cellar. I watched him day in and day out swing the pick into the Oklahoma red clay. Then he would shovel out the clumps of red dirt as he dug deeper and deeper into the ground. The deeper he went, the harder the dirt and the higher he threw the dirt with the shovel.

After the big hole was dug, Uncle George made a roof for it by cutting up a large log the length of the cellar and placing it in the middle. He cut several short logs to go out from the center on both sides. This was covered with a big mound of dirt to keep the rain out. Finally, the cellar was ready for use.

A few weeks later we got our first storm of the season. Of course, it happened in the middle of the night. It was like a living nightmare as Uncle George picked me up and headed for the cellar. Everyone was in a panic as the rain coming down sounded like it was coming through the metal roof of the old farmhouse. The wind was blowing so hard I thought it was going to blow the house away before we could get into the newly built cellar. I was really scared and everyone else looked pretty scared, too.

Grandma, Grandpa, and Uncle George were running around grabbing a few blankets, pillows, a kerosene lantern, and a few other things they thought we might need in the cellar. Uncle George held me tightly in his arms as he ran after Grandpa and Grandma into the cellar. As

Grandpa opened the back door of the house, the wind blew out all the windows in the living room. Glass was flying everywhere. The cellar was about twenty feet from the back door. We ran out on the porch and saw broken-off tree limbs flying and swirling in the air. Uncle George lifted the door to the cellar while he was still holding me. It was raining so hard that I could hardly see anything now...so I just buried my head in his shoulder and held on tight. The wind was blowing so hard he could barely lift the cellar door. Finally he got it open and Grandma and Grandpa ran from the porch into the cellar.

Grandma grabbed me out of Uncle George's arms as she ran down the cellar steps. Uncle George waited until we were all in the cellar before he turned around and started backing down the steps while he pulled the door shut. The steps were made of dirt. He had cut them out when he was digging the cellar. The door did not seal well and water was already seeping in onto the steps. As the door closed, Uncle George slipped on one of the muddy steps and fell backward. But as he fell, he continued to pull the door shut with a rope. At last, we were all safe from the tornado.

Grandpa held the kerosene lantern, which now dimly lit up the dirt room. After a few minutes, he noticed something moving up on the top step close to the cellar door. It was a snake! Grandpa pointed and yelled, "George, look out! Git that snake!"

Our guardian angel must have helped us that night in the cellar because, luckily, Uncle George had forgotten to take the shovel out of the cellar when he had finished digging it a few weeks earlier. He grabbed the shovel and began to chop furiously at the snake with the sharp end. After he killed it, I wondered what else could possibly happen to us.

It seemed like we were in the cellar a long time, but I was only four and had no real sense of time. We could hear the wind blowing hard and objects were banging around outside. The rain was still coming down hard and quite a bit of water was running down the steps into the cellar. The water was beginning to wash away our dirt steps too. Every now and then, Uncle George would climb up and push the door open enough to see what was happening outside, but the raging storm had not stopped.

We looked around and noticed that the whole backside of the cellar was also starting to leak water. By now, the water was up to our ankles and rising fast.

Uncle George said, "It's still a storming' too bad fer us t' go back into th' house." I was so frightened as I watched the water rise up to Grandma's knees. While she held me, Uncle George and Grandpa tried to patch the leaks in the back part of the cellar with dirt they grabbed off the side of the walls. It wasn't working and I was afraid more snakes might come out in the water holes springing up. Uncle George looked out again and said, "I think it's calmed down enough fer us t'run back t' th' house." Grandma agreed and said, "We hafta chance it, 'cause this here cellar is about t'fill up an' cave in on us."

The water was so high that now my feet were dangling in the water as Grandma held me. The water was almost up to her waist. We had another problem, too: the steps had washed away into a big glob of mud. Uncle George tried to climb up the blob that used to be steps and kept slipping down. He jumped up and opened the door and climbed out. It was still raining hard, but the wind had died down. The blankets we had taken into the cellar were all wet and muddy and certainly were not keeping us dry. Uncle George got on his knees and reached down and pulled Grandpa out of the cellar. Then he reached down and pulled me out as Grandma handed me up to him. Grandpa and me headed for the house while Uncle George got Grandma out. Grandpa and I waited on the porch because it was pitch dark in the house.

Uncle George went into the house first and lit another kerosene lamp since the one in the cellar got rained out. Once we entered, we saw glass all over the floor. Since I was barefoot, Grandma took an old rag and wiped glass off the wooden dining table and set me on it. Uncle George had another kerosene lantern lit by now and set it on the table beside me. Uncle George and Grandpa took the other lantern in hand and started checking out the rest of the house for damage. They came back in a couple minutes to report that all the windows were broken out and even our beds were soaking wet. Grandma found some dry blankets in a closet and made me a pallet on a small dry space on the floor. They never went to bed that night. When I awoke the next morning, most of the mess inside the house was cleaned up.

When I went outside, there were tree limbs everywhere and one of the barns for the horses had the roof blown off and was now laying in our front yard. Now that the storm was over, the skies had cleared and the sun was shining brightly onto the front porch where Grandma had laid out all our bedding to dry. My dog Penny was laying on the porch soaking up the sun, too. He had run and hidden under the house during the storm. He sure looked happy to see me and we walked all around the place to look at all the damage done by the storm.

Picking Cotton: A Family Thing

My mother and two sisters came to stay with us. It was cotton-picking time and Mother and Uncle George would go out to the cotton fields about daylight with these big long cotton sacks. They must have been twenty to twenty-five feet long and two to three feet wide, with a shoulder strap on the open end of it that fit over your shoulder. Also, there were big knee pads that Grandma had made and you would put this strap over your shoulder and crawl on your hands and knees with this big long cotton sack dragging along behind you and as you crawled along, you would pick the cotton from the rows on both sides. After you went down one row and back and your sack got full of cotton, there would be a big wagon at the end of the row for you to empty your cotton from your sack and then start all over on the next long row.

When I would wake up, Grandma would fix me something to eat and then I would get my dog, Penny, and go to the cotton fields and just play while Mother and my Uncle George picked cotton. I would only play a short time when I would hear Grandma calling as she walked across the cotton field toward us, telling us to come and eat dinner. Everybody would stop and take their big heavy straps off their shoulder and leave the cotton sack laying down on the ground and head for the house. After dinner, we would go back to the cotton field to pick up where we stopped.

As Mother crawled along picking the cotton, I would help by picking some and putting it in her cotton sack, but sometimes I would pull off the whole cotton boll.

Uncle George would holler at me. "Don't put that whole thing in thar, ya hafta take th' hull off an' jest put th' cotton part in thar."

Then he would take a cotton boll and show me how to just pick the cotton out of the hull because you don't want the hull in with the cotton. Well, I would pick and play and run up and down the rows until I was tired and Mother or Uncle George would have to take me and lay me on the very end of one of the cotton sacks that were kind of full of cotton and I would go to sleep. This was how I took my afternoon nap. I would wake up about time for them to stop for the day, because it was getting too hot for them to pick anymore.

One time I was playing and Uncle George was crawling along picking cotton when I heard him calling for me and Mother to come over. Mother quickly took the strap from her shoulder and we both ran over to him. He was holding the bottom part of his pants leg and said, "I bet ya can't guess whut I have up my pants' leg."

We just stood there and looked at him and after a moment, he said it was a baby rabbit. I got really excited about maybe having a baby rabbit. As Uncle George put his other hand up his pant leg, I stood very still, waiting as he got a hold of it and pulled it out. But it wasn't a baby rabbit. It was a big black tarantula.

I barely got a chance to see it, because the minute he saw what it really was, he threw it across the field. As I saw him throw that big black thing, my mother screamed. I was already scared from seeing it and now her scream really got me scared. Once we calmed down after all that excitement, we laughed at how we thought it was a baby rabbit.

A Step Up from Sharecropping

I was about five years old when we moved from this place to Midwest City, a town just east of Oklahoma City. Uncle George had gotten a job at an apartment complex as a maintenance man where his brother Tom was working. Even though it was just a minimum wage job, which only paid about thirty-five cents an hour, it was a step up from sharecropping on a small farm with just a team of mules. We lived in a duplex on Douglas Blvd. across from Tinker Air Force Base.

We had only lived there a short time when winter set in and there was a lot of snow that year. The highlight of my days was to watch the cars get stuck in the snow on this hill beside our house. No one could make it up this hill and there was a man that had an army jeep that would push each car up the hill. It was fun watching the cars sliding all around trying to climb the hill and then finally the jeep would come and save them. I made friends with Ricky, a boy that lived across a dirt driveway in front of our house. He was about my age and I think he was the first friend I ever had...because living on the farm by Elmore City, there were never any other children for me to play with.

Well, there was this pipe laying beside Douglas Blvd. that was about a quarter mile long that was put there by the gas company. They were hooking it together before putting it in a big trench they were digging. One of us would get on each end of this pipe and talk loudly and the other kid at the other end of the pipe could hear whatever was said. It was like talking on a telephone to us. We would watch cars slide and tell each other what was going on at the other end of the pipe. I guess we were lucky that some car didn't slide off the road and hit us.

I was sitting in my house eating breakfast one day when I heard a lady and a kid crying. I went to the front window and looked out to see my new best friend, Ricky, with his mother and little sister, standing in the dirt driveway crying. All their furniture, clothing and everything was sitting out in the driveway with them. I asked Grandma why they were crying and why were all their things sitting outside in the driveway? It made me want to cry, too.

She explained that this happens when you don't have any money to pay your rent and the owner of the house will come and move all your things outside in the driveway. I asked Grandma if this is what happened to us when we lived in Arizona because Mother said we went to live in a cave after we got put out in the street. Grandma said yes and she was sure glad we were living back in Oklahoma now.

I went outside to talk to Ricky and he was crying and said they had no place to go and that his dad had lost his job and that they didn't have any money. My Grandma came out and talked to his mother. Then Ricky and his mom came into our house and Grandma fixed a big pot of stew, which they ate a lot of because they were really hungry. After a while, Ricky's dad came back and took them away. I never saw Ricky again. All my life, I wondered what happened to him.

School Daze
A short time after that, we moved to a little house about twelve miles east of Oklahoma City. This was the house that my Grandpa would die in and also where we lived when I started first grade. The school bus would pick me up right in front of the house and would take me to the nearby town of McCloud, Oklahoma. The only thing I remember about that first school year was this little girl I met. I don't even remember her name, but I remember that we spent almost all our time together. We would eat lunch together and sit beside each other on the school bus.

She liked to skate and she brought an extra pair of skates to school and we would skate on this patio at the back of the school. She always put my skates on me and buckled them up and then I would do the same for her. She was the prettiest girl I had ever seen and once in a while, we would kiss. One time, some of the other kids saw us kissing and told the teacher and we got in a lot of trouble. The kids would tease us a lot, but we didn't care and we still played together all the time.

Berries Coming Out of My Ears
There was a big blackberry farm across the highway from our house and in the summer, people came from everywhere to pick blackberries. That summer, I decided to try and make some money picking blackberries. I had Grandma take me across the highway and help me get started. They had these wooden trays with a handle on the top. The tray was about twelve inches wide and eighteen inches long and they held six little cartons to hold the blackberries. I would fill up all these cartons and take them up to a wooden shed and they would mark down how many cartons of berries I turned in. Then at the end of the day, I would get paid for all the cartons I had picked.

On the first day of picking, I didn't do too good. I must have been a very slow picker and I guess I ate about as many berries as I picked because, by the time the hot summer afternoon rolled around, I got very sick. One of the ladies at the berry farm had to walk me home across the highway and take me to my Grandma, who immediately saw what was wrong with me. She smiled at the lady and said, "Too many blackberries, I guess?" The lady smiled and said, "I reckon so."

Grandma thanked her for bringing me home, took me in the house, put me to bed in the living room and put a cool damp rag on my head. I went to sleep and did not wake up until late the next morning. The next day, I didn't pick any berries, but that summer I continued to pick berries, and by the end of the summer, I had saved up $6.00 toward buying myself a little wagon. But when we went to town, the wagon was no longer $6.00, but now cost $7.50. Uncle George gave me the extra $1.50. I felt pretty proud of myself because this was the first time I had ever saved up my own money to buy something.

Burnt Shoes

I went to stay with my mother for a couple of weeks in the winter a few days before school was out for Christmas. She took me to the store and bought me a pair of shoes that were brown hi-tops. They came up around my ankles to keep my feet warm. It snowed the next day and Mother had to go to work at the meat packing plant. My two older sisters had to go to school and Mother said I could walk with them. I put on my new shoes and went out in the snow. We went down a little trail for about two blocks and then across a railroad track and then one more long block to get to their school. My sisters told me to go straight home just the same way we came and to stay inside the house until they came home from school.

As I was walking back home, I saw a boy playing by the railroad tracks and stopped to talk with him. He told me he wasn't going to school because he was sick. When I look back on it now, I realize he was just playing hooky, probably because he wanted to play in the snow. He was a couple years older than me, so I thought he was really cool. He told me he had a great hideout down by the railroad bridge.

We walked about a half-mile down the railroad track, kicking snow and throwing snowballs. As we approached a creek, he told me to climb down under the bridge. Big wooden beams held the bridge up. We slid down the banks of the dry creek in the snow. Then he told me to look up. On the right side of the creek bank at the bottom of the bridge was a hole between two wooden beams. He said this was his special hideout.

We climbed under the back of the bridge, which was pretty easy because there wasn't snow under it. We got to the hole and he told me to climb inside. I put my head in this big hole and climbed in. I slid down into the hole until my feet finally touched what I hoped was the bottom. I was afraid to move, but after a while, my eyes adjusted to the darkness and I could just barely see my new friend climbing in the hole after me. He saw I was afraid and told me everything was okay. My eyes had adjusted enough that I could see I was in a dirt cave right behind the bridge beams. Shortly after we got settled, I heard a roaring noise and asked my friend what the noise was. He said he didn't know. By now, the ground was beginning to shake violently and dirt was falling from above our heads. I tried to look up and out of the hole we climbed in, but the dirt was falling so fast that it was getting in my eyes.

The falling dirt got worse and the noise got louder and louder. Suddenly, we realized it was a train coming over the bridge, as the beams were shaking and dirt was falling everywhere. The beams were shaking so much I was afraid to crawl out of the hole between the beams to get out. I think my new friend was as scared as me because he didn't say a word. As soon as the train passed over, I couldn't get out of the hole fast enough. I left my new friend and ran straight home. Never knew his name.

When I got home, I discovered my troubles were not over. All that walking in the snow and sludge had gotten my new shoes soaking wet. I knew I could not face my mother with my new shoes all wet. She worked very hard get me these shoes and in my five-year-old mind, I started wondering what I could do to get my shoes dry before she comes home. If only I had a way to heat them up so they would dry out. Then an idea hit me: I would put them in the oven!

I went over and lit the oven the way I had seen Mother do it and put it on the low setting. Surely this would dry my shoes before she got home. Putting my plan into action, I put my shoes in the oven and closed the door. I was relieved, for now, my problem was solved. I put my old worn-out shoes on and went out to play some more.

Well, I must have lost track of time while I was playing, because I looked up and saw Mother getting off the city bus down at the corner. By this time, I had forgotten all about my shoes in the oven and was just excited about seeing her. I ran down the block and give her a big hug. As we walked back, she asked what I had been doing all day. I still was not thinking about the shoes. I only thought about that horrible experience in the hole down by the railroad bridge and I sure wasn't going to tell her about it because she would get mad at me for doing such a dangerous thing. I just said I had been playing outside around the house.

As we reached the house, Mother opened the door and smoke started rolling out the door. She yelled, "What's burning?"

It hit me like a ton of bricks and I froze while thinking about my shoes in the oven. Mother figured out the smoke was coming from the oven and went straight over and opened up the oven door. There were my shoes ... not on fire...but they were good and dry and smoking. She grabbed a towel, got the shoes and threw them outside into the snow. She went back over to the stove, turned the oven off and opened the back door to help air out the house. Then she just sat down on the floor looking distraught.

I was still standing outside looking in the front door. I didn't know what to say or what to do. Mother just sat there for a while looking down at the floor. After a few minutes, she looked up and asked me to come to her. I went over and sit down by her. I was about to cry, but I knew that wouldn't do any good. I told her that all I was trying to do was dry out my new shoes after getting them really wet while playing in the snow. She reached over and hugged me and told me everything would be okay. But somehow I knew I had failed the test to be able to stay with my mother. In a few days, I was on my back home to live with Grandma, Grandpa, and Uncle George.

Another One-Room House
By the end of the summer when I was seven years old, I was going to get to go live with my mother in Capitol Hill, a suburb on the south side of Oklahoma City. She had a little one-room house that was set back behind a larger house. We had one bed that me, Mother, and my

two older sisters slept in at night. When you walked in the front door, the bed was on the right-hand side up against the wall in the corner. On the left side were a few kitchen cabinets with no sink and no running water. Our water supply came from a pipe sticking out of the ground with a faucet on it, back close to the alleyway. We had a bucket that we would fill up with water and take into the house for all our needs. We also had another bucket that we used for our potty needs in the middle of the night or during bad weather. Mom would never let me take it out back in the alley to the outhouse because she was afraid I would spill it. Everyone else I knew and played with had an indoor toilet. In the back left-hand corner of the room were a little table and two chairs where we ate. As you faced the back wall, there were a couple chests of drawers for all our clothing and possessions. Plus, we had cardboard boxes under the bed for our stuff. We didn't have any closets or a place to hang clothes.

I moved in with Mother and my sisters about two weeks before school was to start. I had always wanted to live with my mom, so this was a really good time for me. I had always lived in the country with no kids to play with and now I was living in a city neighborhood filled with children. There were several boys close to my age nearby.

I had only lived there a few days when a boy from across the street shot me in the leg with his BB gun. I ran across the street, threw him to the ground and jumped on top of him. Sitting on his chest with my knees on his arms, I grabbed both of his ears with my hands, pinning his head to the ground. As I looked around, there were several other boys standing over me and one of them was his big brother. He said to get off him or he would kick my teeth out. I looked at him for a minute and decided to get up. I didn't say anything...just stood there looking at him...but suddenly something came over me and I charged the older brother with everything I had, grabbed him by the neck and threw him to the ground ... His head hit the ground with a thud and it took all the fight out of him. As I sit there on his chest, I told him that if his brother ever shoots me again with that BB gun, I was going to feed it to him.

After that day, I never had any kids in the neighborhood picking on me, and if kids from other neighborhoods came around starting trouble, all my friends would tell them how tough I was and they would *hit the road*. From then on, all the boys in my neighborhood and I were good friends.

Learning To Be a "City" Boy

One day, a couple of kids came over from a different neighborhood and my friend Paul was having a hard time with them. Two other friends, Billy and Clarence, came running up, telling me there were some kids about to kick Paul's ass. We ran across the street and down the alley where I could see Paul standing in the middle of the alley surrounded by a bunch of other boys.

Now, Paul was short like me and stocky-built with blond hair. He had a happy and fun personality and we got along great, never fought. I went running as fast as I could down the alley towards him.

I said, "Hey, Paul, what's going on?" and he just stood there not saying anything. I could tell he was pretty scared. There were about six boys and they were all bigger than us four. I took one look around and knew I didn't want to tackle any one of these guys. One had a real mean look in his eyes.

Billy and Clarence were standing back by the side of the alley. I put my hand on Paul's shoulder and said, "Let's get the hell out of here."

As we started to run away, the kid with the mean look in his eyes stepped in front of me. I had only had a few small scraps with other guys and wasn't really a fighter but I had heard about how these city kids would gang up on you and that some of these gangs were really tough. I was so scared I started shaking but knew I had to do something, so I hit the mean guy as hard as I could. I guess I thought that one hit would scare him away. Because after I hit him, I backed up – raised my fist like I would do it again – but to my surprise, all I had done was make him really mad. He came at me like a wild man. I didn't have a chance and got a beating that day.

I went home and began to think about what I had done wrong. I realized one thing was that I was scared and not mad. There were times in the past I fought when I was mad and was willing to fight no matter

what the outcome. But when I hit this kid, he got mad and I was too scared to fight. I just stood there, so I decided that if I had to fight again, I would get really mad at this boy and go after him with everything I had in me.
As the days passed and I began to heal and continued to think about it, I was beginning to get mad about what had happened to me. About a week had passed and I was doing fairly good by now and most of my injuries had healed up. I got up one morning thinking about how this kid beat me and for no reason and I decided I wasn't going to let him get by with this. I told myself that the next time I saw him I was going to jump his ass! I didn't tell any of my friends what I planned to do.

I had heard my friends talking about him hanging out at the school playground so I asked them if they wanted to go up there. At first, they said no, but I talked them into going. We got there and no one else was there and we were just hanging around sitting on the front steps of the school. I looked up and saw this kid with the mean eyes. A couple of his buddies were walking down the sidewalk. I got up and started walking toward the sidewalk and Paul said, "Hey, what are you doing?" I said nothing and just kept walking.

When I reached the sidewalk, Mean Eyes was about twenty feet up the walk, still walking straight toward me. I just stood there looking down like I was scared because I wanted to surprise him this time. I didn't allow myself to be scared and just kept thinking about what he had done to me. I was getting madder the closer he got to me and when he got about six feet away, I made a run at him and hit him in the face with my fist. I continued to hit him as fast as I could and I must have hit him ten to twelve times before he knew there was a fight going on. By then, the fight was pretty much over. I had knocked him down and I was sitting on him, punching him in the face. Clarence and Paul grabbed my arms and said, "You don't want to kill him, do you?" They pulled me off, after that, all I wanted to do was go home.

On the way home, I could hear Clarence and Paul talking about the fight. I didn't pay much attention to what they were saying because all I wanted to do was go home. I was having some very mixed-up feelings. Part of me was feeling bad that I jumped that kid and another part was feeling good he got what was coming to him. I didn't say a word all the way home because all I could think about was what I had done. I was trying to decide if it was the right or wrong thing to have done. When I got home, I was glad that my sisters were not home and Mother was at work. I didn't want to see anyone. I went in, got on the bed and just laid there until I went to sleep. The next day I had gotten over my mixed feelings and everything was back to normal.

Guardian Angel

The main part of Capitol Hill in Oklahoma City started on the corner of Robinson Street and S.W. 25th Street and encompassed about six blocks on 25th Street. There was a Sears, Montgomery Ward, J.C. Penny, several 5 & 10 stores, a couple of drug stores, an Oklahoma Tire & Supply Store and a lot of Mom & Pop stores. A lot of the main stores like Sears and, of course, the 5 & 10 stores, sold toys. We lived about half a block east of Robinson on S.W. 26th Street.

Living only a couple of blocks from all these stores, I found myself spending a lot of time just going from store to store, looking at everything. I would pick up the toys and play with them until a clerk would come over and tell me to put the toy back on the shelf. I would go home and dream about having some of these toys.

Before I moved to the city and just lived in the country, I didn't see toys or think about them. Even when we would go into town in Elmore City, I don't remember ever seeing any toys in the stores. Out in the country, we did get a Sears Catalog about once a year and it had some pictures of toys in it. Living this close to all the stores was kind of like living inside a Sears Catalog where you actually got to touch the toys. I got to feel what it was like to roll the cars and trucks across the floor and hold the airplanes in my hand and fly them around.

After living in the city for several months, I was still amazed at all the things for sale in the stores. They stayed open late at night, and since my mother had to work the evening shift from three to eleven at night, I had plenty of time to roam the stores. My older sisters were supposed to babysit me, but they were teenagers and were never home, so I was free to roam the streets until it was time for Mother to get home. All the other kids I knew had to be in by dark. I didn't want to go home and be by myself, so I would walk down to the stores and just look in the windows and go to store after store and dream about having all kinds of things. Sometimes the store manager would ask me to leave and I would just go to the next store.

All the stores closed at 9 p.m., so I would go to the drug store because it didn't close until 10 p.m. The drug store had a long bar with several bar stools and sometimes I would go sit on a bar stool and just watch the people come and go. After doing this several nights in a row, a nice lady that worked behind the soda fountain counter asked me if I wanted a soda. I told her no, I don't have any money. She said that's okay, this one is on the house.

"On the house? What does that mean?"

She said it means you don't have to pay for it.

"Boy, that is great!"

The lady smiled and gave me this big glass of soda that had Coca-Cola written on the side.

This was my very first Coke. It was foamy on top and when I think back, I can almost taste that Coke today. It was the best Coke I ever tasted in my entire life. The lady began to talk to me and she asked me a lot of questions about where I lived and why I was out so late at night. She had seen me in the store several times before and I explained that my mother worked until 11 p.m. and that I didn't like to be home by myself. She asked where my dad was and I said I didn't have a dad.

"Is your Dad dead?"

"No, I ain't got no dad and don't ask me about him again."

She quickly changed the subject and asked me if I would like a hamburger. I said, "Yeah, if it's on the house?"

"Yes, it is."

"If I take the burger, are you going ask me more questions?"

She said, "No more questions, we can just be friends."

When she started cooking my burger on the grill, I told her, "You probably don't want to be friends with me, older people don't like me. The only older people that like me are my mother, grandma, grandpa, and Uncle George." She wanted to know what I did to make grownups not like me.

I said, "I don't know, but they just don't like me."

She said, "Well, I like you and you can come in here and talk to me anytime."

I still wonder today why I thought grownups didn't like me. The few parents of my friends and schoolteachers were the only grownups I had been around except for my family. They were never very friendly and I always sensed they were in a hurry to get away from me. Maybe it was because I was so poor. Whatever it was, it caused me to resent and distrust most grownups and rebel against any of their rules.

I would go and see the counter lady three or four times a week and she would give me a coke and make me a burger. I never knew her name or where she lived. I had been going to the store for about six months when one day I walked in and did not see her and there was another lady working behind the counter. I asked what happened to the other lady that worked there, and she said, "She moved away."

I never saw the nice lady again. I always wondered if Grandma had prayed for me to have a guardian angel. My mind will wander back to this time in my life, and I wonder why the lady behind the soda fountain counter was so nice to me. She would feed me and treat almost like I was her child. Then I think about how she disappeared out of my life so suddenly and I never saw her again. Was she my guardian angel?

Santa Is Coming to Town
It was the last part of November and all the kids at school were talking about what they thought they would get for Christmas. I would just walk away and be by myself. I knew I wasn't going to get anything for Christmas. My mother was working at a bakery and would walk a mile to and from work and made only $15.00 a week.

With three kids to feed and clothe and rent for a house to live in, it just didn't leave any money for Christmas presents. Until now, Christmas was just another day when all the family came together for a big meal at Grandma's house. The grownups would visit and I would get to play with all my cousins. I had never thought about Christmas as a day to get a lot of presents. But I had never lived close to other children who talked about bicycles and all sorts of wonderful toys they would get for Christmas. All my prior Christmas Days were held in the country and my playmate was just my dog.

Moving to the big city was so exciting for me. I loved getting to play with other children, but I didn't really love seeing all the toys and things they took for granted, things that I had never dreamed of owning. My favorite store to visit was Sears & Roebuck, probably due to my past experience with the Sears Catalog back on the farm. But there were lots of times I wished I was back on the farm with just me and my dog. That way, I wouldn't have to deal with all the other kids bragging about all their great stuff.

I wouldn't have to fight with other kids, either. When I lived in the country, I always had peace of mind. I didn't worry about what people thought about me. I didn't compare myself to other children. Basically, while I was living on the farm, I didn't know I was dirt poor. So many people could hurt your feelings in the big city in so many ways. However, I still loved the city and decided you just had to take the bad with the good.

So Christmas had come and gone. We had gone to my Grandma's house and had our usual get-together. It was fun seeing all my cousins. But when we got home, I saw all the new bicycles and toys the neighborhood kids had received for Christmas. They were all out playing and showing off their new things. I tried to act like it was no big deal. But inside I was aching...it was a big deal to me!

I started going to the stores even more than before, looking at the toys. The ones I liked the most were the windup cars, trucks, and bulldozers. They all had a spring built inside and when you wound it up, some could run for about twenty feet. My very favorite toys of all were the race cars because they rolled the fastest. I would get the cars off the counter, wind them up, and let them race each other across the floor. Of course, after a while, a sales clerk would come over and ask me to leave.

I'd walk back home and see the other kids playing with all their Christmas toys and feel dejected because I didn't even have one toy. A few days later, I was back looking at toys in the store, playing with a cool wind-up race car. I had been playing with it for quite awhile and was surprised no one came over and told me to leave. I looked around and noticed that the store clerk was busy in a different part of the store. The door was pretty close to where I was playing, and then a thought hit me. I took a good look around to make sure no one was watching. I picked up the racecar and put it inside my coat. Then I just walked out the door onto the sidewalk. When I walked by the big window in front of the store, I just walked normal so I wouldn't draw any attention. After that, I ran all the way home.

Once I got home I knew I had to find a hiding place for my stolen car. Mother would be very mad if she knew I had stolen something. So I started looking around and saw a place where you could get under our rent house. I opened up a wood cover and thought, "Yep, this is the place." I knew a store nearby that threw out wooden boxes behind their store. I ran up there, got me a box and put my car inside. This was where I would keep it.

Now I went around showing off my car to the neighbor kids. Now I had a toy and I felt like my life was getting better. Even when Mother would see me playing with the little racecar, I would convince her that one of my friends had just loaned it to me. This was great. So I decided to go back to the same store and get another toy. I was dying to impress my friends with new toys so much and I discovered it was pretty easy to shoplift. I didn't know it was called shoplifting, but I knew it was stealing.

It wasn't long until I had a box full of cars, trains, airplanes, and trucks hid under the house. In fact, I had to go get more boxes for my stolen toys. I never let the other kids know where I kept my toys, either. If someone was over playing and wanted me to get a certain toy, I would say, "Oh, I left it over at my grandma's house."

This toy thing was going so good that I started to take some of the little toys to school and sell them to other kids. I sold most of them for five or ten cents, but that was pretty good money for a little kid back in the 40s. I thought this was great because I had money *and* toys.
I was becoming popular, too, because kids liked to hang out with me so they could play with my toys. This all went on for about five months until school was out and I had to go stay with my Grandma for the summer.

Just Me, My Dog, and the 1938 Ford

It was back to just me and my dog. This really did seem like a better life for me, not having to worry about what other kids thought about me. I was away from the stress of stealing all those toys in order to keep up my image. I could just relax and walk in the woods with my dog and enjoy nature.

I was eight years old and felt like I was thinking different since I had experienced the big city life. In the past when I was younger, my Uncle George would let me steer the car by sitting in his lap. He had a 1938 Ford and I would just go sit in the driver's seat and pretend I was driving. One day he came out of the house to go to the store and saw me sitting in the driver's seat. I asked him if I could back the car out of the drive and to my surprise, he said, "Yep."

He got in the passenger side and I started the car, pushed in the clutch and used the gear stick that stuck up from the floor between the driver and passenger seat. My legs were pretty short and it was hard for me to hold the clutch and reach over and put the gearshift in reverse. Uncle George just sat there looking at me with a big grin on his face. I could tell he was thinking I said I could do this and he was just going to sit back and see if I really could. Well, I passed the test and backed down this long driveway to the main road.

After that, he would sometimes give me the keys and I would run the car up and down the driveway for hours. By the time summer was over, he had started taking the back roads to the store and letting me drive. I was driving at age eight and was mighty proud of myself.

That summer had its good and bad times. The bad was when my Grandpa passed away and I loved him so much. He was a lot of fun….always teasing me in a good way. Grandma would get mad at him when he milked the cow because he would squirt me in the face, trying to hit my mouth. But mostly he would miss and get my clothes all messy.

He had a couple of strokes and was always okay mentally and could speak afterward, except for the last one. He lived only a few hours after the last stroke and died at home before they could get hold of a doctor. I wouldn't go to the bed and look at him. Grandma was crying so I just ran outside into the woods with my dog, Penny.

After he died, I knew nothing would be the same. I would have dreams about him, once I dreamed Grandpa was milking the cows and he pointed one of the cow's teats at me and sprayed me with milk ... and I just laughed. I remembered how we sat on the porch with Grandpa telling us jokes for hours. Sometimes he would get to laughing so much that we never could understand the joke he was trying to tell us. Other times, he and I would walk together through the corn fields to check how the corn was growing…or we would walk the fence line to see if the fence needed any repairs so the cows would not get out. I had spent a lot of good times with my Grandpa and now he was gone…but he lived on in my dreams.

Making the Country Sparkle

That summer I brought with me some of my new bad habits that I had picked up in the city. Some older boys in the neighborhood setup a fireworks stand about a quarter mile up the road, selling fireworks for the Fourth of July. I would take my dog and walk up there once or twice a day and just hang around. Sometimes the boys that ran the fireworks stand would fire off a few fireworks ever so often just for fun. They were about seventeen or eighteen years old and I was just eight years old, so to get to hang out with these older boys and get to shoot off fireworks was pretty cool stuff.

Grandma was used to me being gone for a couple of hours at a time because I would go for long walks down by the creek with my dog. She didn't know I was spending all my time hanging around with some older boys. At times, there would be twelve or thirteen kids hanging out at the fireworks stand, and I would always be the youngest. Hanging out with the older kids made me feel like somebody important.

Well, it was getting close to the Fourth of July and the boys running the fireworks stand were talking about what they were going to do on the night of July 4th if they didn't sell all the fireworks. They were just going to fire off everything left over. Well, it was July 4th and the day was about over and I really wanted to go down to the fireworks stand in case they had any fireworks left over so I could watch them shoot them off. But I knew Grandma and Uncle George would not approve of me being out after dark. So I had to dream up a plan.

Grandma and Uncle George went to bed about 9 p.m. I waited until I thought they were asleep, and then I climbed out of my bedroom window and went over the fence on the opposite side of the house where the dog slept. I didn't want my dog to follow me, so I ran all the way to the fireworks stand. Not long after I got there, we started shooting off the extra fireworks. There were eight or ten boys ranging from twelve to eighteen years of age, and there was me, age eight.

We set off fireworks for a while. The small firecrackers we had were more powerful than the little firecrackers we have today. They were called Red Devils and were like small pieces of dynamite. You could take just one and put it in a mailbox and it would blow it to pieces. The other fireworks we had were called Roman Candles. We would set these on the ground and they would shoot up and spray out different colors. We had finally fired off everything except for some Red Devils and we had a lot of them left.

One of the boys came up with the bright idea of us all going down by the road where there was a bunch of trees. We would hide in the trees and throw Red Devils at the cars as they drove by. We thought this would be great fun.

We all piled into two cars and headed down there and pulled the cars off the road behind the trees. We got out and got our firecrackers ready for the first car to come by. We heard a car coming and we all got ready to light and throw a Red Devil at the car as it passed by.

When it went by, our fireworks were popping all around the car and we all started laughing and talking about how close our firecrackers came to the car.

There wasn't much traffic on that highway at night so we had to wait ten or fifteen minutes for each car. The cars kept coming and we kept throwing our Red Devils. All the sudden one of the cars lost control and ran off the road and down into a ditch. We all just stayed hidden in the trees watching and wondering if anyone was hurt. We had been waiting and watching for about ten minutes when about five Highway Patrol cars pulled up and a bunch of cops jumped out and started running toward the woods where we were hiding.

All the boys started running all over the place in different directions. I grabbed a tree limb and climbed up in a tall tree as fast as I could climb. When I was up as high as possible, I stopped and looked down. I saw that some of the boys had been caught. The cops had some big spotlights that they were shining all through the trees. The spotlights were shining all around me and I was thinking that at any minute they would see me. They continued to round up the other boys, handcuff them and put them in the patrol cars. I just hung on, trying to be as still as a mouse and hoping they wouldn't see me.

After a while, they had began to give up finding anyone else. Slowly, the patrol cars began to leave and finally the last one drove off. I didn't see anyone around or any cars, but I still stayed up in the tree quite a while just to be sure everyone was gone. While hanging up in the tree, I was wondering if anyone was hurt in the car that went into the ditch. I didn't think they were because I never saw an ambulance come and go.

Well, I finally came down out of the tree and looked around very carefully. I didn't see anyone...but the car that went into the ditch was still there. I thought, "Boy, I better get out of here before somebody comes back to get the car." I decided that I better not let anyone see me walking along the highway back to the road home. I would hide in the ditch every time I saw a car coming. After I got to my road, I ran most of the way back, glad to be home. I climbed in the window to my bedroom, hoping that Grandma and Uncle George didn't notice I had been gone. After I got in bed and got to thinking, I got a little relief thinking if they had noticed, they would be up looking for me. But they were not up.

But now I couldn't sleep, worrying that the cops might come knocking on our door looking for me because one of the other boys might have told them about me. I just laid there, thinking maybe they won't find me since the other kids only knew my first name and didn't know where I lived. I couldn't sleep the rest of the night. For several days, I still worried the cops might come knocking on our door. A few days later, Uncle George read from the front page of the local newspaper about some boys the police arrested for causing a car to crash. It did say no one was hurt in the crash. The boys were still in jail.

For the rest of the summer, I stayed close to home and spent my time just taking my dog for walks down by the creek.

School Starts Again/Crime and Punishment

When summer was over, I went back to Oklahoma City to live with my mother. Since school was about to start, mom told me that I would be going to a different school than my two sisters. We attended a little Pentecostal Church, which only had about seventy-five members. Mom said the church was in the process of building a school and I would be going there this year.

Once school started, I had to ride the city bus about a mile to school. I got on the bus about a half block from my house and it stopped and let me off right in front of the church. The little school was right behind the church. The schoolhouse was only half finished, with only the first floor finished, the second floor was in the making. The first floor had three classrooms and there were only fifteen students in all. We ranged from the first through the twelfth grade. We had one classroom that was large enough for all us students. Most of the time we only had one teacher and all the students were in the same classroom.

I didn't learn very much since all the grades were mixed together and the school wasn't very organized. Our teacher was the preacher of the Pentecostal Church and not formally trained in education. None of the students took this school seriously; even the teacher would sometimes be gone for an hour or two and leave one of the older students in charge, which was a joke. We had a lot of fun, but I don't think any of us learned very much. Sometimes the "Preacher-Teacher" would give us something to do or study in class ... we all knew he just gave us busy work because it was his nap time. A few minutes after he gave us a paperwork assignment, we began to hear him snoring. We'd look up and see him with his head back and his arms hanging down to his side. He looked like he was about to fall off his chair.

That was when the games began. We would take rubber bands and paper clips and start shooting them at each other. This really hurt when you got hit. I guess we were lucky nobody got hit in the eye and of course, the spitballs began to fly, too. Well, one day I had this three-ring binder with the back and front I torn off. All that was left was the middle metal part with no paper in it. I was sitting at my desk opening and snapping it shut. Then an idea hit me. This smart-ass kid sat in front of me and was always making me mad. I leaned forward and snapped the metal binder on his ear. He started yelling and jumping all around the classroom with this metal notebook binder clipped on his ear and blood was flying everywhere. The class was screaming and going wild, watching him bleeding and jumping around.

I was in shock. I wanted it to hurt, but I didn't know it was going to pierce his ear and hurt so much. I watch the boy in disbelief. Then, I happen to look up and see the teacher standing up from his desk. He looked like he was half-awake and wondering if he was having a nightmare. He was a big man, standing about 6'2" and about two hundred and twenty-five pounds. Once he woke up and realized this was not a nightmare and that he was really seeing a boy with a notebook binder clipped to his ear with blood everywhere, he looked like a madman. By now one of the other students in the classroom had settled the boy down enough to get the metal binder unclipped off his ear.

I look up and see the teacher coming my way and I knew I really screwed up this time. I had never seen a grown man look this mad before in my life. Once he figured out that I was the one that had caused all this commotion, he was looking around for something to paddle me with. But when he didn't see anything, he just took off his shoe and started hitting me all over with the heel. He was so upset at me that he was hitting me on the head and shoulder and anywhere he could make contact with my body. I really didn't blame him for being so mad at me, because I deserved everything I got and probably deserved more. That was a very dumb thing I did and I still wonder what made me do something so stupid. I learned a good lesson that day about stopping and thinking before doing anything.

Monarch Roadmaster for Streetwise Kid

As time went on, I became more and more adjusted to the city life as a poor kid. I was stealing toys, candy, clothes and shoes, and anything I could use or sell so I could have a little cash. I got caught stealing a few times, but all they would do is take me to the back of the store and talk to me. They told me I would go to jail if they caught me stealing again. That didn't stop me; I would just avoid that store for a while. There were plenty of other stores for me to steal from. I would go into a shoe store barefoot and slip on a pair of shoes. When no one was looking, I would just walk out of the store.

Mother asked me where I got my new clothes or shoes. I told her that some nice lady a few streets over gave them to me because her son had outgrown them and after I had worn things for a day or so they would look used. She never suspected anything. Maybe she was too busy trying to survive as a single mother to notice.

Christmas was coming up and Mother said she wasn't going to let her children go through this Christmas without a nice gift. A week before Christmas she got me and my two sisters together and walked us over to the Oklahoma Tire & Supply Store, about two blocks from our house. I loved this store because they sold bicycles. She went over and picked out a bike called Monarch Roadmaster. It was the most expensive bike in the store. She told the clerk that was the one she wanted and she filled out paperwork to buy the bike on credit.

She had to make payments of $5.00 a month. I knew my mother was only making about $15.00 a week and it would be hard for her to make all those payments. So I promised her I would find a part-time job and make the payments. And I did get a job at a car lot about a half block away from my house. I cleaned cars in the summer and shoveled snow in the winter.

We headed home with the bike. I had to push it because I didn't even know how to ride. My sisters didn't know how to ride a bike, either. I learned real quickly, but my sisters had a harder time. My oldest sister, Mazella, tried a few times and didn't like it and just gave up trying. My other sister, Ozella, broke her arm trying to ride and gave up, too.

The bike was supposed to be for all three of us but ended up being all mine and I kept my promise to my mother and made all the payments. I didn't get to work at the car lot a lot. I only worked there a couple times a month, so I had to make the rest of the money stealing and selling things. But the New Year started off great with a new bike that I could ride to school.

Mother was working evenings, so after school I explored all kinds of places in the city on my bike that used to be too far to walk. Within a couple of months, I was riding to downtown Oklahoma City at night and discovering a whole new world of stores with lots of new things to steal. None of my friends had the freedom to roam the city because their parents expected them to be home by dark. So I became a loner and enjoyed my freedom. Since I was alone, no one knew what I was up to and could tattle on me.

One morning, I started to school and decided to go to a nearby school on my bike and see if some of my friends went to that school. I left my house early so I could be at the school early. When I got there, I planned to take out my two really neat windup racecars. I figured when my friends saw me with them they would want them and might buy them from me. I arrived early but nobody was there. I sat down on the front steps of the school and waited for my friends to arrive.

As they came walking up to the school, they started shouting out at me, "Floyd, what are you doing at our school?" "Are you going to our school now?"

I said, "Nope, I just came by to show you my new cars." I reached in a bag I had on my bike and pulled out two racecars.

They said, "Boy, this is just what I have been wanting!"

I said, "Yeah, I know...that is why I traded for them yesterday...what will you give me for them?"

They could only come up with fifteen cents, but I sold them anyway because I needed some money. The school bell rang and they had to run into the school. By now, I realized I was still a mile away from my school and I was going to be late. But the closer I got to my school, the more I realized how late I was going to be. Finally, I decided not to even go to school that day. I just rode my bike around town, but was afraid to go into any stores because I thought some grown-ups would ask me why I was not in school.

In Love with Movies

As I rode around downtown Capitol Hill, I saw two movie theaters and a thought hit me. I had never been to a movie before, because my mother believed it was a sin. She had told me that if I ever went to a movie, I would go to hell. I wanted to believe what she told me, but I just couldn't see what was wrong with going to a movie. I looked at the movie hours and saw that one opened at noon. It was almost that time, so I just sat on my bike in front of the theater waiting for it to open. I waited until a few people went in before me then went up to the movie window to pay for my ticket. It cost me one dime.

After I went inside, I went to the concession area and bought a popcorn and coke for a nickel each. That would be my lunch for the day. I went in and sat down, waiting for the movie to start. I forgot to notice what was playing, but then it started and I saw that it was going to be a western. The movie began with a bunch of men riding horses and robbing a stagecoach and there was a big chase and lots of shooting at each other. I was spellbound as I watched my very first movie.

After I got home that evening, I just acted as if nothing was different. However, the next day came and I knew I had to go to school. What was I going to tell the teacher? I decided I would tell him I was sick since I knew he wouldn't see my mother for a few days later at Sunday school. I was hoping he would forget about it and not say anything to her. Sure enough, nothing was said at Sunday school and all was well.

After that, I started to miss a couple of days a month and would always tell the teacher I was sick. Everyone at school seemed to accept that I was a little sickly and nothing was said to my mother. I was in love with the movies. All I ever did when I ditched school was go to the movies.

Mother Is Missing

My older sisters had already dropped out of school. They didn't want to follow any of Mother's rules and argued a lot with her. My next to the oldest sister, Ozella, would even physically fight with my mother. I was too young to know what to do when they started fighting, so I would just leave the house for a while. My oldest sister, Mazella, was sixteen years old and had a boyfriend that my mother did not approve of and they would argue about that a lot. Mother was also under a lot of stress at that time, working long hours to provide us all a very meager way of life. Four people living in a one-room house was not easy.

One night around 10:30 p.m., Mother was due to come home, but 10:30 came and went with no Mother showing up. I wasn't very worried because sometimes she would have to work an hour or two of overtime. I was so tired that I laid down and went to sleep. I don't know if my sisters went to sleep that night or if they stayed awake waiting for Mother. Anyway, at 4:00 a.m., they wake me to tell me Mother had never come home. They told me to get up and get dressed. As I put on my clothes, all I could think about was what had happened to my mother. Had something bad happened to her? I started crying and that started my sisters crying. They told me to hurry and finish getting dressed so we could go look for her.

I said, "Where are we going look at this time of night?"

"We are going over to the neighbor's house and ask them what to do."

Our little house was back in an alley behind a larger house. We walked out of the house into the dark. It was a very dark night. One of my sisters started crying again, saying that Mother could have been kidnapped while walking home in the dark. By now, I had got past my crying and decided I wasn't going to cry anymore because it wasn't going to help me find my mother.

We walked up onto the front porch of the house in front of ours. We knocked on the door very hard until someone came to the door. My two sisters were crying uncontrollably by now. They asked us to come in and my sisters told them that Mother had not come home from work. Our neighbor didn't have a phone. We didn't have a phone. So all we knew to do was to go back to our little house and wait for daylight. Daylight comes and still no Mother. By now, I was in a state of shock. All I could think about was what my sister said about Mother being kidnapped. I didn't want to think that way, but the thought kept popping up in my mind and I started to tear up again.

I bit my lip and told myself that crying would not solve the problem. I forced myself to think up other reasons she was not home. Maybe she was still at work and couldn't call because we didn't have a phone.

By now, our neighbor had left for work. He said he would call some of the church members from his work. In a couple of hours, some church members showed up and told us they had checked the place where Mother worked and she had left work the night before at 10:00 p.m. They had notified the police and had filed a missing person report. A few minutes later, the police showed up and they wanted to talk to me and my sisters. They started asking all kinds of questions that I didn't want to answer. Questions like: "Were any of you fighting with your mother?"

I ran back into the kitchen part of the house and one of the officers followed me. He continued to ask me all these personal questions...and I just refused to answer him. He asked me what I was hiding. This made me really mad and I told him to go straight to hell.

"I ain't answering any more of your stupid questions!"

I turned and walked over to a kitchen window and stared out as he continued to ask me questions. I didn't say a thing and after a while, he gave up on me and went back in the living room. I just kept staring out the kitchen window until I heard the door slam and he had left. I went back into the front part of the house and my two crying sisters hugged me and told me we're going to find our mother. I couldn't cry now because I was so mad at the cop for asking all the dumb questions. I resented him asking questions about my family and the church people.

Questions like—"What are you and your sisters going to do? Where are you and your sisters going to stay while you wait on your mother to come home?"

The neighbors helped out by bringing over some food for us, but I wasn't hungry. I didn't want to stay in the house and just sit around and think about what happened to my mother. I knew I had to get away. I just needed to go anywhere so I could get all this off my mind. So I told my sisters that I wanted to go stay with Uncle George and Grandma. The church people were the only people I knew that had a car. They agreed to take me to Uncle George and Grandma's house.

When we arrived and I told Grandma what had happened, I could tell she wanted to cry. Instead, she just grabbed me and hugged me and told me everything would be all right.

"Yer mother will be back soon."

After the church people left, Grandma fixed me some dinner and we didn't talk about Mother. She found other things to talk about in hopes of keeping Mother off my mind. Grandma went to clean out the hen house and I took my dog for a walk in the woods.

It was great to be back with my dog, Penny. When I moved to the city, I had to leave him on the farm with Grandma and Uncle George. Penny loved the country and would never have adapted to city life—but I sure did miss him. When Uncle George came home from work, Grandma told him about Mother.

For the next several days we didn't talk about her at all. Every day, I would take long walks in the woods with Penny and try not to think about what happened. Sometimes I couldn't help thinking about Mother and would just sit down by a tree in the woods and cry, sometimes for an hour or two. Penny always came and sat by me. He would lick the tears from my face. I don't know how many days passed; I think it was about five or six days and still no word. Grandma and I didn't know that Uncle George was driving all the way into Oklahoma City every day after work, checking on my sisters and hoping for a word about my mother.

Sunday morning, he decided to take me and Grandma to Oklahoma City to check on my sisters again. We had only been there for about thirty minutes when I looked out the window and saw my mother walking down the alley toward the house. We all ran out the door and down the alley to meet her. After a few minutes of hugging, everyone started asking her what had happened to her. She told us she was all right but refused to talk about where she had been or what had happened. To this day, no one in my family knows where she went or what she did those days she was gone. We were so happy to see her back that we didn't push for answers.

I thought the real reason Mother left was due to her being stressed out from fighting with my two sisters, working hard late nights to support us, and still many times not have enough money to feed us. Sometimes the church people would bring us food. I think we all learned that we needed her in our lives. We appreciated her more and my two sisters didn't fight with her as much. Mazella didn't give up her boyfriend that Mother disliked so much but Mother gave in and didn't try to stop her from seeing him.

My dog Penny died not long after Mom's disappearance and return. I really was sad when I lost him, but maybe my Grandpa's death had prepared me for the loss of Penny. I don't think of animals as guardian angels, but Penny was my best friend, companion, and playmate. He was always at my side when I went into the woods and I guess you could say he was also my babysitter and protector. I pretty much went out in the woods with Penny whenever I could just for fun and to avoid facing unpleasant events.

I loved Penny but I loved my Grandpa more than words can say and miss him to this day. Maybe he became my guardian angel or at least an advisor to my guardian angels to help me through what was to come later in my life.

Things went along fairly good for the rest of the school year. All my family was getting along better and I had a little money to go to the movies when I skipped school. School had only been out for a couple of days when Mazella came home and said she was getting married. She was only sixteen years old. I could tell that Mother didn't like this at all. But she resigned herself to accept that Mazella was getting married. Six months later, my other sister, Ozella, decided to get married, too. She was barely fifteen years old.

Then it was just me and my mom. I knew things would be great now because Mom and I never argued. We got along great. I tried my best to please her because I saw how hurt she was when my sisters disappointed her. The summer was about over and we still lived in the little one-room house in Capitol Hill. It was pretty cozy with just the two of us.

Boys Will Be Boys and Girls Will Be Girls

One day I made a big mistake when I went out to play. Mother was at work and all my buddies were gone somewhere and I was kind of lonely. These two girls came over from across the street and asked me to play with them. At my age, it wasn't cool to play with girls but since there weren't any boys to play with, I agreed to play with them. We tried playing marbles and a few other boy games but that wasn't working very well. We decided to play house and I was the dad and one of the girls played the mom and the other girl was the daughter. The girl's mom had cooked up some brownies and she had gone to town and nobody else was home so we decided to go in the house and eat some of the brownies. Once we were inside the house, I sat down, and the oldest girl served us some brownies, as we were still playing house.

We were having fun eating brownies and playing house and then the pretend mom and dad decided to kiss. We kissed a couple more times to make the pretend games seem more real. We were kissing a lot pretending we were married. Somehow I knew grown-ups didn't like for kids to kiss and play house the way we were doing that day! I admit we took playing house a little too far. I was a little worried about our little escapade, but I had no idea what the next day would bring.

The next day was Sunday. Mom and I got up and got ready for church. We had to walk about two blocks and catch a bus that took us to church about two miles away. I was still thinking about what happened the day before. At church, I prayed that God would forgive me and thought that no one would ever know what happened. Boy, was I wrong!

We had just returned from church when someone knocked on our door. Mother opened it and three ladies stood there looking very mean and said, "Mrs. DeBurger, we need to talk to you about your son." They asked if they could come in and one of the ladies said, "Sonny Boy ... you need to run along outside and play while we talk to your mother." I didn't like an outsider telling me to leave my own house and I wanted my mom to say *this is our house and he doesn't have to leave unless he wants to*. But she was intimidated by these women. I looked back at her as I went out the door, hoping she would say something. She didn't say anything to me. I left and shut the door behind me.

I knew one of these women was one of the girls' moms. But I didn't think they would know about me and the girls playing around. How could they know? Surely the girls didn't tell and no one else knew anything about us messing around and kissing. But I was wrong! One of the girls had talked. I never knew which one, because I was forbidden to ever see either girl again. The next few days would let me know that I was not welcome to play with any of the boys or girls in my neighborhood. These women continued to come by our house and have private talks with Mom. I did the one thing I didn't want to do: burden my Mom with more worries. I sure caused a big problem for Mom, but what happened could not be turned back.

This problem took me a long time to get over. Mom and I decided we needed to move since we were never accepted in the neighborhood due to my shenanigans. People already looked down on Mother because she was a single mom. They looked at her as a scorned divorced woman and treated us like white trash.

We found an old apartment house that had four apartments downstairs and a fifth apartment in the attic. As you walked in the front door of the apartment house, there was an apartment on each side of the hall. Then as you walked down the hall, there was a stairway that took us to our attic apartment. The hall was barely wide enough to squeeze by the stairs and on the right under the stairs was the bathroom that everyone in the entire apartment house shared. That was fine with me because that was better that using an outhouse and it had a bathtub in it. I couldn't wait to try out the tub, as I had never taken a bath in a real bathtub. Always before, I just used a washcloth and soap in a bucket of water and would wipe myself down to get clean.

Once we passed the stairs and bathroom, there were two more apartments on each side of the hall close to the back door. I went back to the stairs and took one look at them and thought I better be very careful on these stairs as they looked like they were made from used lumber. Whoever built the stairs built them in a hurry, too. When I stepped on the steps of the stairway, they rocked back and forth every time I went up and down them. I thought they might come crashing down any minute. Once we reached the top of the stairs, we were in our apartment, which was just a big open attic room without any door. If I heard someone coming I would just walk over and look over the rails to see who it was.

When standing at the top of the stairs, Mom and I could stand straight up there and in the middle of the open room. But the attic walls slanted on the sides, so everywhere else we walked in the room required us to stoop over to accommodate the slanted ceilings. We had two little half beds, one for me and one for Mom. For the first time in my life, I had a bed of my own. I had to be careful when rising up in bed or I would hit my head on the ceiling. I really liked living in this little attic apartment, just me and my mom.

A Tree House with TV

I thought of the house as a tree house like I would have built myself with all the different angles in the ceiling and the little bay windows that I would have to get on my knees to see out. For the first time in my life, we had running water in the kitchen. The kitchen was not another room, it was just some cabinets along one wall with a gas stove on one end and a refrigerator on the other. We used the burners on the stove for heating the place if it was cold out. We had to wear our coats in the house to keep warm. It was a fun place to live, with neighbors that liked me.

The people that lived to the south of us owned a furniture store and I thought they were rich because they had a television. I had seen a television in the stores before but I had never watched one. My new friend's parents owned the furniture store and I would watch Hopalong Cassidy on TV at his house. His mother was real nice and she would fix us snacks to eat while we watched TV. She would also invite me to eat with them a lot of the time when she knew my mother was working late. We had only lived there for about ten months when mother's friends from the church told her she could live in their old house since they had just built a new one. The old house was not very nice but at least it was free rent.

There weren't many kids to play with in this new area where the old house was located. I would just ride my bike around the neighborhood and over to Capitol Hill to the stores, which was about two and a half miles from my house. I would spend hours going from store to store, looking at the toys and stealing a few. And I would take them to school the next day to sell them. I had some friends at school but they never invited me over to their house. I guess they thought I was too poor and they would never come over to my house, either. But we had a lot of fun at school.

The next few weeks, things were going really good. I was just riding my bike and hanging out with my friends, not knowing that the next few years were going to be pure hell.

Preacher-Man Comes to Town

It all started when we went to church one Sunday evening and we listened to a visiting preacher that was holding a revival for one week at our church. All the people in the church really liked his preaching. Usually, my friends and I sat in the back row during church services talking and acting silly...until whoever was preaching would stop and tell us to behave and be quiet. But when this new preacher, named J.D., preached, my friends and I would be still and listen. He was very dramatic. Sometimes he would dance across the stage and get very loud and work himself into a big sweat, then take out a handkerchief and wipe the sweat off his forehead. Then he would stand still and talk real soft and slow.

We were mesmerized; it was like he put a spell on everyone in the church. Nobody said a word, you could hear a pin drop when he paused. With other preachers, people in the audience would be talking during the sermons...saying *"Amen," "Yes Brother"* or *"Praise God."* But when J. D. preached, everyone was quiet as a mouse.

J.D. was about 5'10" and weighed around two hundred fifty pounds. To me, he was a large person because my Uncle George and Grandpa were not tall or heavy men. He had a nice-looking face and was always clean-shaven. He dressed real sharp for his day and time, with a suit and tie. Apparently, he was going bald, as he shaved his head, too.

Uncle George said J.D. strutted around *"like a banty rooster."* None of my mother's family liked him and thought he was a smart-aleck-know-it-all-big-mouth. I don't think it was physical attraction that won over my mom but the fact that he was a forceful preacher. He was smooth, convincing and so strong-appearing that no one questioned anything he said.

After church on the very first night of the revival, he came over and introduced himself to my mother. I was very impressed with him, so I went over and said hi to him before I went outside to play with my friends. Usually, Mother would visit after church for about ten minutes and then we would head home. But this time, all my friends had left and I went into the church building to check on Mom and she was still talking to J.D. I grabbed her hand and said, *"Mom, it's time to head for home. I'm hungry."*

As we walk home, I noticed Mom was in a real good mood. We had to walk about three-quarters of a mile and she talked all the way home. Usually, she didn't talk much on our walks home. It was always me asking questions and her answering them. But this time I didn't get a chance to say anything.

Whenever an outside preacher came to town and held a revival, we would go to church service every night for a couple of weeks. During this time, Mother was working the day shift, so we went every night. On the third night of the revival, J.D. noticed we were walking home and offered us a ride and the fact that Mother accepted his offer was very odd to me. Because in all my life, I had never seen my mother give any man the time of day. After her bad experience with my dad, she had always said all men were worthless. Just accepting a ride home with him made my day! Because I had seen other children who had a dad in their lives...it made me think of how much I would like to have a dad, too.

He drove a 1939 Mercury, which I thought was a fantastic car. As we rode home, I could see a sparkle in my mother's eyes. I liked what I saw and on the way home, I was thinking how good it would be to have money, a nice car, and be able to live like other people in a nice house. We arrived home and Mom told J.D. goodnight. We went in the house and for the rest of the evening, all Mother could talk about was J.D. How he was such a good preacher, what a nice man he was and how he was different from other men who had tried to talk to her.

Normally, during past revivals, I would not go every night to church. But I always had to go to church with Mom on Sundays. This week was different because I wanted to go with her every night. I was interested in seeing what she thought about J.D. On the fourth night, he took us out to eat after church at a little cafe on S.W. 29th Street. I had never eaten out at a real sit-down restaurant before, just soda fountains. J.D. told me I could order anything I wanted, so I ordered a hamburger with french fries and a coke. I remember that night very well. Everything seemed wonderful, like a dream. However, it wasn't very long after that when things began to change and I would wish it was back like it was with just me and Mom.

The rest of the week, every night after church we would eat out at a drive-in or restaurant. Then J.D. would take us home in his fine car. I had never seen my mom in such a good mood and talking all the time. On Saturday I got up and went for a ride on my bike and got home around two in the afternoon. J.D. was there and we all went for a ride out by Lake Overholser and had a picnic lunch. For the next week, the pattern was pretty much the same: going out to eat after church and then going home. The last two weeks of my life had made a big change. I hadn't been going to Capitol Hill to steal toys or running around late at night on my bike.

I came home one Sunday afternoon at the end of our two-week whirlwind of church meetings, car rides, and eating out experiences to find J.D. in my house with Mother. She told me to come in and sit down because she wanted to talk to me. She was very serious so I didn't say anything. I sat down and J.D. proceeded to tell me that he and Mother were getting married and we were leaving in a couple of hours for New Mexico, where they would be married and stay for a few days.

Later on, Mother and I would discover the real reason J.D. wanted to go to New Mexico to get married was because he was still married to two other women, one in Texas and one in Oklahoma. The preacher was a bigamist!

J.D. had to go to the church and see the pastor for some reason, so we didn't leave for New Mexico until it was almost dark. We drove all night because Mother refused to stop and stay in a motel with J.D. until they were married. Then the Mercury had a problem with the headlights going off and we found ourselves going down the highway and couldn't see anything. J.D. stopped and got out to see if the shoulder of the highway was okay for us to pull off the road. He told me to get out and watch for any car coming, which was not a problem because we seemed to be the only car on the road that night. We sat on the side of the road for about thirty minutes and then the lights came back on. We would drive for a couple of hours and then have to stop again for thirty minutes. This went on all night long.

We finally arrived in Clovis, New Mexico around 2 p.m. the next day. Mother and J.D. went straight to the courthouse and got married. That night we rented a motel room. The bungalow had a living room, small kitchen, bath, and a separate bedroom. I slept on the sofa. We stayed for a couple of days and did some sightseeing. Then we headed back to Oklahoma City. When I went back to school, all the kids wanted to know where I had been and I got to tell them all about my trip to New Mexico and everything I got to see.

The Honeymoon Is Over
We had only been back about a week when J.D. took a revival assignment at a little church in northwest Oklahoma for a four-week period. I checked out of school and we went to this small town called Waynoka, Oklahoma. I checked into school in Waynoka, thinking that going to a different school every few weeks would be fun and adventurous. I was only nine years old at the time and had spent most of my school years in the Pentecostal Church School in south Oklahoma City and really had not learned much in the way of academics. Now I was going to be changing school every month or so. This would turn out to be a bigger disaster for my education than the lousy church school.

Then, on top of all of this came a big change in J.D. He was no longer Mr. Nice Guy, but became Mr. Grouchy, yelling at me for everything I did or didn't do. He expected me to wait on him all the time and tried to control me every minute of the day. One day I started out the door to go ride my bike and he came to the door and yelled at me not to slam the door. It wasn't like I meant to slam the door. It was an old screen door that had a spring on it that was so strong that it was actually hard to open. If you didn't hold on to it until it was completely shut, it would slam hard. He yelled so loudly at me, I could still hear him yelling a block away as I rode off on my bike. I yelled back "Okay" and kept riding around.

Waynoka was so small that it only had about ten blocks each way, so it didn't take me very long to look over the whole town. I had only gone to school for a couple of days and didn't know any of the children that lived there. As I rode around, I didn't see any kids out and about so I decided to ride back home. We were staying in a house that the church was finishing up for us while we were living in it. When I rode up in the yard, J.D. came running out of the house and, as I climbed off my bike, grabbed me by the arm and dragged me into the house. Once inside, he pushed me down on the sofa and told me not to get up until he said so. I had no idea what he was mad about. He went into the kitchen to get himself a glass of water and came back and just stared at me.

Then he said, "Don't think your mom is going to stop me from teaching you a few rules."

"What rules are you talking about?"

"You do whatever you want to whenever you want to and from now on, whenever you leave this house, I want you to tell me where you are going and when you are coming back! I think it has been a long time since you have had a good ass beating and if you don't follow the rules, you are going to get one."

I sat there on the sofa for a little while and then Mother came back in the house. I found out later that J.D. had asked her to go visit a lady in the church. I wondered where she was while he was yelling at me. I sure was glad she wasn't there because I didn't want Mother to be unhappy and worry about me.

City Boy Goes Back to the Country

The following weekend we were invited out to a church member's house in the country for dinner after church. We ended up staying the rest of the day. There were three boys that were older than me, with the youngest being about one year older. After dinner, the boys wanted to go fishing. Even though I had lived on a farm with Uncle George and Grandpa, I had never gone fishing, so I thought this would be great. We gathered up some old cane poles and some fishing line. We all took a piece of line and tied it to the cane pole and attached a hook to the end of the line. Then we grabbed an old wooden box full of dirt with worms in it and headed down to the creek.

This brought back memories of when I lived with Uncle George, Grandpa, and Grandma. I would take my dog and go down to the creek and just sit and throw rocks in the water and listen to the birds sing for hours. Once we got to the creek, the boys showed me how to put a worm on my hook and drop my line in the creek. I sat down and waited. As I sat there and waited, I began to think about how my life had changed. Now I no longer liked to sit by the creek quietly. I had gotten used to living in the city with so many things to do. I tried to talk a few times but the boys told me to be quiet or I would scare away the fish. I sat there as long as I could stand it, then I told the boys I was bored and thought I would go back to the house.

The oldest boy said, "Hey guys, the city boy is bored so why don't we find something exciting for him."

One of the other boys asked me, "Do you know how to ride a horse bareback?"

I said, "You mean with no saddle?

He said, "Yes."

I said I never rode a horse before because when I lived on a farm we only had mules. They all said, "Come on, we'll show you some real fun!"

We headed back to the barn and they got a bridle for each one of us. We all headed out into the pasture to find the horses. We walked at least a couple of miles down a dirt trail made by wagons going across the field. The horses came right up to us as soon as they saw us. The oldest boy pointed out which horse I would be riding. I didn't know why he picked this particular horse. The horses all looked the same to me. He helped me put on the bridle and told me to just hold the reins until they all got their horses bridled up. Then he helped me climb on the horse's back. We all rode our horses bareback on the dirt trail and everything was going great for about two minutes. I was riding along behind everyone else and then all the sudden my horse thought he was in a race and took off like a racehorse. He passed everyone, leaving them in a trail of dust. With no saddle and just the reins to hold on to, I grabbed some of the horse's mane along with the reins and hung on for dear life. I felt like my entire body was flapping in the breeze.

The horse went down the creek bank, through the creek, and up the bank without even slowing down. He was in full stride as we headed down the dirt trail and I was wondering where the boys were and why they were not trying to stop this runaway beast. I was afraid if he slowed down he was going to start bucking like in the westerns in the movies. So I thought maybe it was better if he just kept running until he wore down and wouldn't have enough energy left to buck. I looked up and saw the barn up ahead and thought this is good! "If he throws me off, I'll be close to the house and someone will hear me when I yell."

I also saw a fence between us and the barn. The horse was in full stride now, heading straight for the fence. I got set for him to jump the fence, wondering if I could hold on or if I was going to bite the dust. I looked up one more time and the fence was right in front of us. I tightened my grip on his mane and the reins and squeezed my legs as tight as I could on his belly. Then, to my surprise, he took a sharp left turn and I didn't, but instead went flying over the fence and hit the ground hard enough to knock the breath out of me.

I landed on my right shoulder and it really hurt. I thought I had broken it but managed to sit up, still gasping to get my breath back. I remember trying to holler for some help but nothing came out of my mouth. After a minute or two, I was able to breathe again. I tried once again to holler for help and right then the other boys came riding up on their horses and they ask me if I was all right. I wasn't going to let these country boys think this city boy couldn't handle a little bareback horse ride, so I stood up and turned to face them when the oldest boy jumped off his horse and started yelling at me as he was climbing over the fence.

"We have to get you back to the house, you're hurt bad!"

Still trying to be tough, I said, "Hey, I'll be all right in a little while," not knowing that the back of my head was bleeding badly and that my shoulder was bleeding, too.

He said, "You're bleeding all over."

He turned to one of the younger boys and told him to go get my mom and dad. He ran over and grabbed me, then yelled at me to sit down.

"I ain't going sit back down, I want to walk up to the house!"

I could see the house was about a hundred yards away. One of the boys jerked his tee shirt off, handed it to me and told me to hold it on the back of my head.

I said, "Why, is it bleeding that badly?"

"Yep, you have blood running all down your back!"

When I started walking toward the house I could see both sets of parents running across the field toward me. When they got to me they took one look and said, "We better take him to the doctor!" The boys' dad said that the closest clinic was in Woodward, Oklahoma, about four miles away. He went to get his pickup because it could get across the field faster than a car. He told my mom and J.D. that he would take me to the clinic and that they could follow in their car. The boys rode in the car with Mom and J.D. Turns out my injuries were not very serious, but I had a hole in my head just above and behind my right ear from landing on a rock. They X-rayed my shoulder and it wasn't broken. I did have a cut on my shoulder that was caused by the barbed wire fence. The doctor gave me some painkillers for my headache.

By the time we got home, I was doing fine except for the big place on my head they had shaved and taped up with gauze. For a few days, I was pretty sore, too. I healed up fairly fast in the next few weeks. This was good because after several weeks, we were moving again to another small town for J.D. to hold another revival. We only stayed at each place for two or three weeks at a time. I was beginning to think that moving around all the time was not so much fun after all. Having to meet new friends and start over all the time was not what I expected it to be. Also, I was not getting along with J.D. very well. He still wanted me to wait on him all the time and didn't let me have any time outside of the house.

Slam-Damn Preacher Man
One day he had sent me to the store to get a few things from a grocery store about four blocks away. My bicycle was broken so I had to walk. I didn't goof off on the way to the store and on the way back. I didn't run or get in a hurry, I just walked normally. As I came walking up to the house, J.D. comes out of the house yelling at me, "What took you so long?"

I said, "Nothing, it just takes that long to walk to the store and back."

As I got closer to him he hauled off and hit me so hard that it knocked me down. This was the first time he hit me, so I was really caught off-guard and surprised.

He said, "Get up, you big baby, I didn't hit you that hard. Just get out of my sight. I don't want to see you again today!"

I got up and started walking away, still dazed from the hit. My head was hurting and I was so mad I could have bit through a nail. I thought about getting a club of some sort and sneaking up behind him so I could hit him back. Then I thought about the possibility of not hitting him hard enough and he might be so mad he would kill me with the club. I put my hand on the spot that hurt the most and felt a big knot on my cheek just below my eye.

I began to wonder what Mom and I had gotten into. I noticed that she hadn't been so happy lately, too. Then I began to wonder if he had hit her. I said to myself, "If I ever see any him hurting Mom, I'll kill him!"

Sunday Matinee

I walked around for about thirty minutes, thinking about what I would do for the rest of the day. I put my hand in my pocket and realized that I still had the change from the money J.D. had given me. I decided to walk to town and check out what was playing at the movies. But I had to be very careful trying to go to the movies because Mom and J.D. and all the members of the church he preached at believed movies were sinful. I didn't want any church member to see me buying a ticket and going to the movies. They might tell J.D and I would be in big trouble again. Also, he would make my mother think I was a bad boy, too.

But I decided to take a chance because I really wanted just a few hours to take my mind off of what had just happened to me and I hoped a lot of the horrible feelings would be absorbed by the movie. I walked by the movie house very casually, glancing to see what time the movie started and at the same time looking around, checking to see if anyone from the church was nearby. The movie started at 1:00 p.m. and it was only five minutes after twelve noon. I check to see just how much money I had in my pocket, $1.26 and the movie only cost a dime. I had plenty of money to get me a burger before the movie started. I looked around and saw a drugstore across the street and it had a soda fountain that served soda and hamburgers. I made my way across the street and went into the drugstore and climbed up on one of the barstools at the counter. I ordered a burger and coke. It cost me only twenty-five cents. By the time I finished my burger it was time for the movie to open up. I made my way back across the street, checking all around to see if anyone was watching me. I bought my ticket and hurried inside. Once inside, I could relax for a few hours. It was a double-feature movie and I sat through it twice. When I left it was almost 8:00 p.m. I headed home, knowing that Mom and J.D. would be at church until 9:30. I would have a little more time before all hell would probably break loose again. I go into the house and lie down on my bed. I must have fallen asleep pretty fast.

All of the sudden someone had me by the arm, jerking me out of bed. I looked up and saw it was J.D. He pulled me up real close to his face, staring at me and said, "Where did you go last night boy?"

I glanced out the window, see it is daylight and realize it is the next morning. I answered, "You said you didn't want to see me, so I just walked around town for the whole evening."

He said, "I don't know what you have been up to...running around in the dark all night. Also, I don't want you telling your mother that I put that bump on your face because I didn't hit you that hard...so if you go around telling lies like that to her, I can hit you a lot harder than I did."

I didn't say anything. I just sat and stared at him. He said, "Don't give me that look or I'll knock the hell out of you again!"

I got up and went into the kitchen. I realized I had slept in my clothes all night. I went to the icebox and got me a glass of milk and sat down at the table. Mom came walking out of the bedroom and asked me if I wanted something to eat and at the same time noticed the whole side of my face was black and blue with a big knot on my cheek. She runs over to me, "What happened, Floyd?" I looked at her and then I looked at J.D. and just stared at him for a minute. Mom asked me again in an alarmed voice, "WHAT HAPPENED TO YOU?"

I paused for a minute and said, "I was playing baseball and got hit with the ball."

Mom said, "J.D., you need to take him to see a doctor."

I jumped up and said, "I don't want him to take me anywhere," and I ran out of the house. J.D. followed me out into the front yard and grabbed my arm and said, "You better watch your mouth, boy."

I said, "Go ahead...hit me again, I can handle it!"

He just squeezed my arm really hard and stared at me. That was because he knew Mom was standing in the front door looking at us.

I told him, "Someday I'll get you back for this, I promise!" I jerked my arm away from him and ran down the street. Once I was out of his sight, I started crying.

Peace—Harder Than War

I headed up to the school, as today was Sunday and I knew I could go sit on the back steps to be alone. I wanted to be alone and think for a while. I began to think about my mom and wonder if she knew what was going on between J.D. and me. Wonder if it would be good or bad for her? I thought back to when she had to work for a living and walked to work because there weren't buses going to her workplace. She would walk to work in all kinds of weather...even if it was raining, snowing, or bitter cold. I remember the times when we didn't have any food for a couple of days at a time because we were waiting on Mother to get paid. Then I thought about the shacks we had lived in, with no running water and outside toilets. I had always been embarrassed for my friends to see where we lived.

I sit there thinking maybe things would be better between me and J.D. I needed to just give it more time and maybe I needed to try harder. I didn't want to go back to what we had before, so I decided I could take the yelling and even a hit once in a while. The longer I sit there thinking, the more I convinced myself that this is the best way.

I decided to head back to the house. I took a detour of a couple of blocks so I could walk through town on the way back home. I took my time, looking in the store windows and day-dreaming about having enough money to go in and buy anything I wanted. As I walked through town, I looked up and saw the town clock on the square. It was 1:30 in the afternoon...I had missed Sunday school and I knew Mother didn't like me to miss Sunday school. I didn't like to displease her, but what was I to do? I couldn't go back in time and change it. I had to go home and face her. I opened the door and walk in. Mom was standing in the kitchen doing dishes from dinner. I just stood there looking at her face for a minute and she asked me, "Where have you been? Why did you miss Sunday School?" I didn't have a good answer for her, so I just stood there looking at her.

J.D. said, "Answer your mother! Boy, you look guilty. What kind of trouble have you been in now?"

I look over at him and I guess I gave him a dirty look because he reached out and grabbed my arm and said, "Don't look at me like that unless you want me to take a belt and beat your ass."

I just stood there glaring at him..... as to say, "I hate you!"

Mom asked, "Did you get that knot on your face from fighting again?"

I didn't answer her. I looked at her and then turned and stared at J.D. I could tell by the look on Mom's face that J.D. had convinced her I was beginning to go bad. I had skipped church, and I was sure J.D. had told her I got the mark on my face from fighting. J.D. turned loose of my arm and said, "I'm going to let you off the hook this time. But just remember, I owe you an ass beating."

Silence Hurts
I went into my room and sat down on the bed so I could think a little bit. I wondered about why I didn't just tell Mom how I really got my black eye and the big knot on my cheek. Maybe it was because I was afraid of J.D.? No, that wasn't it, I was not that afraid of him. Besides, I could take a hit ... it would only hurt for a little while and the pain went away pretty quickly. Maybe it was because I was afraid of what J.D. might do to my mom when I was not around or what he might do if I said anything. Also, would she believe me or him?

When she met J.D. and he took an interest in her, she was overwhelmed. She never had a strong self-image in the romance department. So when she had the opportunity to marry a dynamic educated preacher, she thought she had achieved her ultimate dream. And at that time, she had an almost fanatical attachment to the United Pentecostal Church, idolized preachers, thought they were perfect and could do no wrong. She had a personality that was easily conned and fell for sob stories, too. While she was in that church, she followed the strict beliefs for women: they were to be in submission to their husbands and let the husband make all the family decisions. She could not wear makeup, pants, have short hair or shave her legs. She could never wear a bathing suit or shorts in the summer.

With J.D. being a preacher, Mother believed everything he said. I'm not sure why I didn't say anything, I just knew for the last several days, whenever I thought about J.D. hitting me, I got so mad at myself. I wasn't mad about not speaking up to my mom.

I was sitting on my bed for about thirty minutes when J.D. stuck his head in my bedroom door and said, "Your mom and I are going for a ride in the car and I want you to finish up the dishes and clean up the entire house while we are gone. From now on, it is your job to clean the kitchen after supper every day and on the weekends to clean the kitchen after every meal and straighten up the rest of the house."

I figured…*well if this is what it takes to make him happy, I will do all these chores.*

The next morning I got up kind of late and had to hurry around the house in order to get to school on time. Nothing was going right for me, because the faster I tried to go, the faster the clock seemed to go. I got about two blocks from school and I heard the tardy bell ring. I didn't want to walk into the classroom late because the other students would stare at me, especially with my face all black and blue. Then I would have to explain what happened to me to the teacher and I wasn't ready for that. Besides, I couldn't tell the truth. I couldn't make up a story about having a fight with another student because the town was so small everyone would figure out I was telling a lie. Anyway, we were only going to be in this town for one more week so it wouldn't hurt for me to miss a day.

I talked myself into not going to school. But my first thoughts were that I had to be very careful and not get caught by J.D. and Mom. Sometimes they drove around town during the day, so I had to watch out for their car. I didn't have to worry about many people in town recognizing me since we were so new in town and had only been here for a couple of weeks. I just had to keep my eyes out for anyone from church that might know me, or anyone that might ask me why I wasn't in school. Now that I had gotten all that worked out in my head...I thought I would go down to the bicycle shop and see what a chain and two sprockets would cost.

The Oklahoma Tire & Supply Store sold bikes and parts in the front part of the store and had a repair shop in the rear. I went in and explained to the clerk what kind of bike I had and that my mom bought it at another Oklahoma Tire & Supply store in Oklahoma City. He went in the back and came back with two sprockets and a chain and laid them on the counter. I asked him how much it would cost and he said $6.25. I only had seventy-five cents so I had to do some quick thinking.

I said, "Just leave it on the counter while I go back home and get some more money." I walked over and pretended I was looking at the new bikes on my way out of the store. Just then someone called the clerk to go out back, behind the store, to look at some tires on his truck. I went over to the counter and saw he was very involved in the sale of the tires. So I picked up the chain and two sprockets and walked out the front door and down the street.

The minute I got to the alley, I turned and ran as fast as I could until I was about a half block from my house. I looked to see if the car was home and didn't see it. I went down the alley behind the house and lay the chain and two sprockets in some tall grass. Then I sneaked up to the front door and knocked really loud. I ran around to the side to see if my mother was coming to the door. She didn't, so I knew that nobody was home. I went in and got my tool bag and ran out the back door to pick up my bike. I pushed it down the alley as fast as I could. I remembered an open lot at the end of the town with some shade trees. I thought this would be a good spot to fix my bike because it was enough out of the way.

Later in the afternoon, my bike was fixed and it was good to be able to ride it again. I rode it for the rest of the day. I headed home about the same time school let out and that evening everything went pretty good. Even J.D. seemed to be in a good mood. We went to a hamburger joint for supper. In fact, everything went pretty good for the rest of the week. I had gone back to school and told everyone that I crashed on my bike. Everyone believed me, and it explained why I was absent from school on Monday.

I came home every day and did the dishes and straightened up the house just as I was told. Mother would come into the kitchen and start helping me but every time she did that, J.D. would come into the kitchen and get her, saying, "We need to go visit so and so and pray with them." This would happen every night and they would not come home until after dark.

Moving Around Like Gypsies

We moved at the end of the week. We just went from town to town, sometimes staying in a motel and sometimes staying with church members in their homes. I liked this better because J.D. didn't bother me very much when we stayed in other people's homes. We moved around so much, going from town to town as J.D. held revivals, that I don't even remember the names of all the towns. I would start a new school every few weeks. I would be a total stranger in every new town and every new school, not knowing the students or teachers. With every move, I became less and less interested in school.

Every new school I attended required me to prove myself to the boys by fighting. As time went by, J.D.'s temper would flare up more often, too. He would hit me about two or three times a month. I would have a bloody nose, busted lip, or a black eye. I remember the first time he hit me in front of my mother. We had this old fan. When J.D. sat in the living room, he had to have the fan blowing on him. He always asked me to get the fan and set it on a chair in front of him. When I plugged the fan in, it didn't work and he started yelling at me, saying, "What did you do to this fan? It was working just fine yesterday!"

I tried to tell him, "I didn't touch the fan since yesterday." He jumped up out of his chair, yelling that I broke the fan.

Mother was in the kitchen cooking and when she heard the yelling, she came and stood in the doorway looking at us. When J.D. saw her, he calmed down for a moment and started walking toward me shaking his finger at me, not seeing that I had the cord to the fan pulled tight across the room. He caught the cord with his foot and jerked the fan out of the chair onto the floor. This made him so mad that he just lunged at me and hit me so hard that I was knocked up against the wall. Before I had time to run or even move, he grabbed me with his left hand and hit me again. As I hit the floor my hands and feet were moving as fast as they could, scrambling to get to my feet and run out the front door onto the front porch. I heard my mom yelling at J.D. so I turned around and ran back in the house, thinking that he had hit her. But he hadn't hurt her.

She was in his face, yelling at him for hitting me. She looked over at me standing in the doorway with my nose and mouth bleeding. I could see fire in her eyes as she turned toward him and took a swing at him with her hand. J.D. grabbed her hand, just holding both of her arms for a few minutes. I had to hold myself back from running and jumping him. But my common sense kicked in, telling me that I wasn't big enough or strong enough to keep him from hurting Mom. I would just make matters worse. I turned and went back out onto the front porch and sat down on the steps. I began to think perhaps one of these days I would have kill J.D. Just then Mom came out with a warm washcloth and began to wipe the blood from my face.

She said, "Go get in the car and I'll get J.D. to take you to the doctor."

Mother couldn't take me because she didn't know how to drive and didn't even have a driver's license.

I said, "No, I ain't going anywhere with that madman."

She said, "What if something is broken? How about I go get Mr. Freeman?" He lived down the street and went to our church.

I said, "Mom, I'll be okay. I heal up fast, ain't the first time I've been beaten."

She said, "Yeah, I know but you need to quit fighting other boys so I don't have to worry about you coming home with your face beat up all the time. You know there are ways to solve things without fighting."

I turned around and looked at her, not saying anything. I'm thinking maybe she really doesn't know that J.D. is the one putting all these bruises and bumps on my face and body. She began to tell me how J.D. had been under a lot of pressure lately because he was trying to get his own church. That was why we were traveling around so much. He was looking for a church to hire him as their full-time preacher.

"He just ain't been himself lately," she said. "I'm sure things will get better soon, especially after he gets a church and we get to stay in one place."

I didn't have the heart to tell her that he was meaner than the devil himself. She was blinded by all that so-called religion he preached and she believed everything he said because he was a preacher of the Word of God! Mother went back into the house and I got on my bike and just rode off. Riding my bike was good therapy for me. As I rode around, I thought Mom is wrong: things are not going to get better. Every day is getting worse and there is nothing I can do to make things better. I just have to live with this nightmare.

As I rode my bike, I thought back to the first two weeks after we met J.D. Everything was great, he was taking us out to eat every day, buying me clothes, giving me spending money, and I thought he would make a good dad. When I stole the bicycle chain and sprockets, it was the first time I had stolen anything since Mom and J.D. had gotten married. Now I was back to stealing and skipping school.

I hated school more than I ever did before I met J.D. Being a preacher's son was not as great as I thought it would be. Instead, other kids would make fun of me and tease me. I got their attention when I was new at school and they would tease me about being a preacher's kid and I would say, "Go to hell and shut up or I'll beat the shit out of you." They sure weren't expecting a preacher's kid to talk like that!

Sometimes this tough guy routine would work and I didn't have to fight. But usually, in every new town, there was always someone waiting to take me on. It got to the point where I could look into another boy's eyes and tell immediately if I was going to have to fight him or not. After so many moves, if I saw the look in their eyes, I would just surprise them and jump them before they had a chance to jump me. I had learned that when you surprise someone with a good hard hit that stuns them for a few seconds, you could follow that up with several good punches and win the fight before they even really knew they were in a fight.

Most of the kids I fought were bigger than me, and big bullies that liked to pick on short kids like me. Once in a while, my surprise attacks didn't work and the big bully would beat my ass like J.D. did on a regular basis. By this time I was used to being knocked around, so it didn't really seem so bad if I lost a fight now and then. Whenever I went to a new school and had my big first fight, a few kids would think it was cool that I took on the schoolyard bully and would become my new instant friends.

When I was nine years old I started seeing little imaginary people after receiving multiple beatings from J.D. I see now that this was my child's way of surviving the beatings and not going crazy. These little people were toy-like miniature kids and all were little boys. They would play with me, mostly in an outdoor setting. We'd play with wind-up cars and all sorts of toys. The boys were so happy and fun to play with and sometimes I would carry them around in my hand or my pocket. We would go outside and build little roads in the dirt for the windup cars, trucks, and other vehicles.

They were all little bitty boys and I was the only big boy. I could close my eyes at any time and they would appear and seem so real. I didn't have to be sleepy or asleep for them to appear. I just had to shut my eyes and they would appear. The little boys were never serious or sad but always ready to have fun and play games with me.

They would talk to me but it was always about playing with toys. I never saw them when J.D. was beating me, as I was too concerned with trying to avoid the next blow and figuring out how to survive. It was after the beating was over that I could see them and any other time I wanted to see them.

After I ran away from home and wandered around to different places, I still had my little people with me until I was about fourteen and starting high school. It was like all of the sudden they were gone and it really made me sad, as I missed the little boys and playing with them so much. I don't remember if they had names but I remember they all knew my name. Even today I sometimes wish I could still see and visit my little people.

If Only They Knew

By the time I was ten years old, Mother had been married to J.D. for about a year. It had been the worst year of my life. I used to think that being poor and living in shacks was bad, but now I wished I had back my life of poverty without J.D. But I knew that wasn't going to happen, so I wished I could just go to the same school for a whole year and have the same good friends and really get to know my teachers. So many times, whenever I went to a new class, I didn't know what the teacher was teaching because I had missed out on so many fundamental teachings by attending the unorganized church school and moving all the time.

The first three or four times we moved and I had to check myself out of school none of the teachers seemed to understand my helpless situation. Instead, they would lecture me about how was I going to learn anything if I kept changing schools all the time. Didn't they understand that I didn't have any control over how long we stayed in each town? I would stand there and take their stupid lectures so I could get my paperwork to take to the next school.

At the next school, it was the same questions and lecture about how I was going to have to work really hard to pass with the grades I brought in on my paperwork, and why did I move and change schools so much? I got sick and tired of hearing the same questions and lectures, so after about my fourth move, I didn't bother to check out of school when we moved. When I went to check in at the next school, I would just say the other school is mailing my paperwork. I knew I would move before the "expected paperwork" didn't arrive.

Finally, school was out for the summer. Lucky me, now I would have more time to take care of all the things J.D. came up with for me to do. I was hoping I would have a little time just for myself. Boy, was I ever wrong about having any leisure time! By the time summer was over, I was so happy for school to be starting so I could get away from J.D.

The Great Escape and J.D. Slave

I didn't know I was going to be his slave for the entire summer. One of the chores I had was to keep his car clean. This meant I had to wash it twice a week. After I completed the washing, I had to endure a ten to fifteen-minute inspection by J.D. If he found a little water spot or someplace on the car not shining...he would point out the spot and say, "Come here, boy, do you call this clean?" If Mother wasn't around, he would backhand me across the face. But if she was watching, he would say, "I owe you one!" Then we would move to the inside inspection of the car. He would open all four car doors and start looking under the seats, in the ashtrays, and on the dash.

One time he found a bristle from a hand broom on the car floor and he went ballistic and started yelling at me to come and look at what I left in the car. I didn't come to him because I knew he would hit me. I just stood there. He backed himself out of the car really fast because he was mad at me and hit his head on the metal doorpost. He was really mad at me now. I took one look at him and knew he was planning to beat the hell out of me, so I took off running.

I grabbed my bike and rode off as fast as I could. I looked back and saw him standing in the yard, yelling, "Run, you little bastard, I will get you later!" I stayed gone until I was sure that he and Mom had gone to bed. I knew that the next morning they were getting up early and going to a preacher conference for two days. I also knew that the beating J.D. had for me would not be any easier. In fact, it might be worse, but I thought it was worth trying to put it off for a few days.

I rode up and laid my bike down as quiet as possible. I didn't see any light on, walked around the house and put my ear up to the window to see if I could hear anyone. It was very quiet and it was probably about midnight. I walked very quietly around to my bedroom door. My bedroom was really just a screened-in porch with a bed, so it was easy for me to sneak in and out of the house. I opened the door very slowly and tiptoed to my bed. I lay there trying to think of a way not to be there when they got up. Finally, it came to me: I would leave them a note that I was going to help Henry, my friend, deliver newspapers. I would tell them I would see them when they returned from their trip.

I knew that Henry was always at the station at 5 a.m. getting his papers folded and ready to deliver. I got up at 4:30 and placed the note on my pillow and headed out to the paper station. Since I hadn't made any arrangement with Henry, I thought I would just get to the paper station early to make sure I caught up with him. I thought it best that I went with him on his paper route since I had put that in my note. Besides, I didn't have anything else to do so early in the morning and didn't want to get caught lying and get into more trouble. I was standing outside the paper station when Henry came up and said, "Hey, what are you doing out at this time in the morning?" I told him I just wanted to ride with him on his paper route if that was okay with him.

He said, "Sure, I could use the company." We went inside the station and got his papers and started folding them in kind of a flat circle.

Henry let me hook one of the paper bags on my bike and we headed down the road, throwing papers on front porches. I took one side of the street and Henry the other. I was just learning and had to get off my bike numerous times to make sure the paper went on the customer's porch. We finished up and I told Henry I would see him later and headed for home. I thought if we ever got to stay in a place for a long time I would get my own paper route.

As I rode my bike closer to home, I started wondering if Mom and J.D. had left yet. I had enjoyed working with Henry on this paper route so much that I had temporarily put out of my mind all the trouble I was in with J.D. I began to wish I had already taken my punishment. Thinking about it going to happen was almost as bad as getting the beating. I rode down the street we lived on and saw that the car was gone and a big relief came over me. Then I wondered if maybe they had just gone to the store and hadn't really left yet. I decided to put my bike in the backyard just in case they came back, I could run out of the back door of the porch, jump on my bike and escape down the alley.

As I went in the back door of the porch, I saw a note on my pillow that my mother had left me. *"I got your note so I'm not worried about you. There's plenty of food in the icebox for you while we're gone and here's a dollar for spending money, but don't tell J.D. I gave you this dollar. We'll be back in a few days. Please, don't get into any trouble."*

I sit down on my bed and think about how nice it will be not to have to listen to J.D. for a couple of days. However, I know when he returns I am going to get a beating. I try not to think about the beating for now...instead, I sit on my bed and try to think of all the things I can do while they are gone. Then I think, *"Uh oh! What if they forgot something?"* So I went in the living room to watch out for their car. I made myself a peanut and butter jelly sandwich and sat in a chair close to the front window so I could have a good view of the front of the house where J.D. always parked the car. As I was eating my sandwich, I start thinking about all the things I don't have to worry about now he is gone for a few days.

I don't have to get the newspaper off the porch for him every morning before I go to school. If it ever rained and the paper got wet, it was always my fault so I had trained myself to wake up every morning at five so I could get the paper as soon as it hit the porch. If it ever got wet, I would get knocked around by J.D. If Mom was out of the house, it wasn't unusual for J.D. to walk up to me and hit me, knock me to the ground and put his foot on me to hold me down while he hit me more with his leather belt.

He had to hold me down because I would always fight back or run. If I ran away, I never came back until I was sure Mom was home. If he was home, I always had to get him his coffee each morning. Most of the time he would be mad at me because his coffee was not hot enough or the cup was dirty. Then I would have to bring him his shoes or just sit in the living room with him in case he needed anything. If he didn't like anything I did, there would always be a head-slapping or sometimes an all-out beating.

He also had me doing repairs and outside chores. Every place we lived, I had to clean out the water cooler because it wasn't cooling good enough. I don't think cleaning it helped, but J.D. liked to keep me busy. If he got mad and broke a window, I would have to scrape out all the putty, get the window ready for the new glass and putty it into place. I had to be careful not to break the new glass or I would get beaten up. He broke at least two windows every month. He also had me pulling weeds around the fence and the house.

By this time I was sure they were not coming back for a couple of days. I planned to hang around with Henry and go to a couple of movies. But I had to go to the movies alone because I was afraid J.D. would find out and tell Mom. So I would go to the movies at a different time than Henry. I didn't want anyone I knew to know I went to the movies.

The two days went by really fast. It was time for Mom and J.D. to return home. It was time for J.D.'s revenge. It was about six in the evening when I saw the car pull up in front of the house. I didn't go out to meet them. I just sat there waiting for them to come in the house. Mom came in first, happy to see me and ask how I got along. J.D. came in and didn't say a word to me. He just stood there and stared at me and I just stared back at him. Finally, he said he was surprised to see me at home. "You must have forgotten I owe you one!" I sat there looking at him for a minute and then he said, "Don't sit there looking at me like that! If it wasn't for me, you would not have anything to eat!"

The words just popped out of my mouth. "Go to hell!"

I don't know why I said that to J.D., I guess because I knew I would get a beating anyway. J.D. turned his head, looking for Mom, hoping she had heard what I said, but she had gone back to her bedroom.

J.D. yelled, "Did you hear what this kid just said to me?"

Mother didn't answer him.

"Go out to your room and sit on your bed until I am ready to deal with you!"

Then J.D. stomped off to the bedroom and started telling my mom that he was not putting up with a kid cussing at him. "I'm going to beat his ass!"

Beat your ass' was his favorite saying. I think I heard it at least a thousand times.

My mother said, "You ain't going to whip him again."

"Well, I'm not going to put up with that boy telling me to go to hell!" Mother told him he might need to change some of his ways instead of always wanting to whip me. They began yelling at each other and I couldn't stand to hear them anymore so I went outside and got on my bike and rode off. I rode for a little while and when I came back, my mom had gone over to the church building, but J.D. was still there when I walked in the door.

He said, "Don't think your mom can protect you. I will beat your ass anytime I want to."

He reached his hand behind the door and pulled out a big board. I thought about running out the back door and out-running him. But I knew the beating would just come later. I had learned that thinking and worrying about when it was going to happen was worse. I had been through this ordeal about three times a month for a year now. I was tired of running and just wanted to get the beating over with. But again I opened my mouth and words just seemed to pop out.

"Go ahead you old S.O.B. and beat the shit out of me," I said as I walked toward him.

When I got close enough, he swung the board and hit me across my leg and almost knocked me down. When he raised the board back to hit me again, I ran at him, trying to grab the board. He hit me with his fist and knocked me down. "So you want to fight. Get up and we will just see how tough you are!"

I started getting up slowly and he came over and hit me with the board across my back. He continued to hit me on my back, my butt, and my legs. When he stopped hitting me, he said, "Maybe this will teach you to do as you are told!" He turned and walked out the front door.

I tried getting up and realized my left leg hurt so bad that I could barely move. I managed to get up and hobble out to the back porch and lie down on my bed. As I lay there, I got madder and madder. I didn't feel sorry for myself anymore. I was just mad. Getting mad seemed to keep me from hurting so bad. I lay there thinking that someday I would be big enough to take the board away from J.D. and beat the hell out of him. Then I thought that idea wouldn't work because I would be dead before I got that big. I knew where he kept a couple of guns and thought maybe I could get one and shoot him. Not to kill him, just shoot him in the legs and make him suffer and maybe shoot him in both arms and just stand back and watch him suffer.

I knew I could never do this because I didn't want to go to jail for the rest of my life. But just thinking about hurting J.D. made me feel better. However, I knew I had to think of a way out of this hell. I was only ten years old and could not imagine living like this until I was sixteen or eighteen… old enough to be on my own. That time seemed like the rest of my life. I had to think of something else pretty quick.

After I lay there for a while, I decided to get up and go to the bathroom and check out my wounds. As I got up, I realized my left leg hurt more now than it did when it first happened. I knew it was time for Mom and J.D. to be at church so I wouldn't have to deal with them fighting about me. I still didn't think he had ever hit my mom, but I thought if she really knew what he did to me she would start yelling and go berserk. I was so afraid that would make him mad enough to hit her, too.

So I was really glad they were gone for a while. I managed to get to the bathroom and look in the mirror. The right side of my face was swelling up and turning blue. This had happened to me so many times before that I knew it was really going to look bad by the next morning. I pulled my pants down and there was a great big knot on the side of my left leg just below my hip. I didn't know if I was hurt bad or not. But I didn't want to tell anyone. My back felt like it had lumps all over it. I hurt too much to take my shirt off and look at it in the mirror. By now my leg hurt so bad that I couldn't put any weight on it. I could hardly pull my pants up because my leg had swollen up so much that it made my pants really tight. Finally, I managed to pull my pants up and hobble on one leg back to my bed.

I started to lie down but noticed blood on my bed. I had been lying on my back. I sat on the edge of the bed and started to pull my shirt off. I managed to get one arm out of the shirt sleeve and pulled the shirt around and saw the back of the shirt had blood all over it. I slowly put my arm back in the sleeve of the shirt, trying not to hurt my back doing it. I got an old raggedy blanket from a shelf on the porch and laid it on my back. I kicked my shoes off and layed down and pulled an old sheet over me. I must have fallen asleep very fast because the next thing I knew it was morning.

My guardian angel must have taken care of my pain that night because I slept really sound. I woke up early in the morning with the sun shining brightly through the window into my face.

New Day, Same Pain

As I got out of bed, I could feel my shirt and blanket were stuck to my back. The blanket came loose from my shirt fairly easy. I folded it and hid it under the edge of my bed. I started to take my shirt off. My back and shoulder were so sore it made it very hard to get one of my arms out of the shirt. Once I got one arm out I started to pull the shirt loose where it was stuck on my back. I finally got the shirt off but my back started to bleed again. I found an old towel and went outside to the water hydrant and wet the towel and hurled it onto my back. The cold water on the towel helped my back to quit bleeding.

I went back in the house and put on a tee shirt and a regular shirt over it, hoping that no one could see what happened to me. I got the blanket and towel and put them in the garbage out by the alley. I went back in the house and no one was up, so I just sat on my bed looking out the window, watching the sun. The heat from the sun helped my aches and pains feel better. I heard Mom and J.D. talking, so I knew they were getting up. I didn't want to face them, so I slipped out the back door and got on my bike. I started to climb on it but couldn't get my hurt leg over the crossbar. I just pushed the bike down the alley. My left leg was hurting so bad that I could barely walk on it. But enduring the pain was better than facing them.

I pushed my bike down to the nearby park and just sat down on a park bench for a while. I began to get hungry and I headed back to the house, hoping Mother and J.D. had gone somewhere. I walked up and saw the car was gone. I leaned my bike up against the house and went in the back door. I could hear Mom in the kitchen. I walked in the kitchen door and she looked at me and said, "What happened to you?" and she ran over and hugged me. A hug was not what I needed with my back hurting so bad, but I didn't say anything. I wanted to tell her...I wanted to tell her the whole story about J.D. I don't know why...but I couldn't tell her.

She looked at me and asked, "Have you been fighting again?"

I didn't want her to think all I did was fight, so I told her, "No, Mom, I crashed on my bike and hit my head on a rock."

"When J.D. gets back I want him to take you to a doctor."

"No, Mom, I don't need to go to a doctor."

"But the whole left side of your head is black and blue and your eye is blood red. Can you see out of that eye?"

"Yes, Mom, I can see and I really don't want to go to a doctor. I just want something to eat."

"Okay, but if your eye starts bothering you I want to take you to a doctor."

Finally, summer was over and I was glad that school was about to start. This had been the worse summer of my life. I would just get healed up from one beating and then I would get another one. Some beatings were worse than others. Sometimes J.D. would just hit me with his fist and sometimes just slap me with his open hand. But the hits were always hard enough to knock me down. Then I would scramble to get to my feet and try to get away from him. Sometimes that worked for me and other times he would grab me before I got up and really beat the hell out of me. I was so glad school was about to start because it would give me more time away from him.

Class Dismissed

Just before school started, J.D. got a letter from a church in Hobbs, New Mexico, they wanted him to come and be their pastor. So we loaded up our belongings and moved to New Mexico. They had a parsonage next to the church for us to live in that was very nice. After we had been there a week, it was time for school to start. I got up early and got ready for school. I was very excited about the nice house we

were living in and the prospect of making some new friends at school. I remember Mother telling me that after J.D. got his own church, things would be better. Maybe this was an answer to my prayers.
I headed out in a better mood than I had been in a long time. I got to school and enrolled myself. It was the usual routine now: I enrolled and checked out myself whenever we moved. Mother and J.D. never went with me. It only took a few minutes to check in and find out my class schedule. I used to get nervous when I started a new school, but I had done it so many times that it didn't bother me anymore. I had only attended a couple of classes before it was time for lunch recess. The lunch bell rang so I got the lunch Mother had made me, went to the cafeteria and ate as fast as I could so I would have more time on the playground.

I had only been out on the playground for a few minutes when I heard a car horn honking. I looked up and it was Mom waving at me to come over to the car. I walked over and noticed a trailer behind it. It looked like all of our belongings were packed in it.

Mom said, "Get in."

I asked, "Why? Where are we going?"

J.D. said, "Get the hell in the car and shut up."

I knew something must have gone very wrong at this new church. I didn't know where we were going and didn't dare ask any more questions. I just sat there in the back seat of the car and looked out the window. I was thinking about what the teacher and principal would think when I didn't show up for my classes, as I didn't get a chance to tell any students or teachers I was leaving school. Maybe they would send the truant officer to the parsonage looking for me. As I sat in the back seat of the car, I wondered where we were going this time.

We drove all afternoon and stopped in Midland, Texas, and spent the night in a motel. The next morning, a couple of preachers came to the motel to talk with J.D. He told me to go outside while he talked to the church brethren. After they left, I could tell that J.D. was really angry. I didn't say anything and tried not to do anything to set him off. He yelled at me to get everything loaded up in the car. By now I knew just how he wanted it loaded. I had to hang his suits on a rod in the back seat just a certain way with his white shirts. He had four suits that had to be hung on special hangers and two shirts to be hung between each set of suits. Mother packed all our other belongings in suitcases and I would load them. J.D. went for a walk while I loaded everything. While he was out on his walk, I asked Mom where we were going this time.

She said, "I reckon we are going to Oklahoma City. But I'm not sure." Well, she was right. We went straight to Oklahoma City. J.D. had church contacts there where he could find some preaching jobs. We always went back to Oklahoma City when J.D. couldn't find a preaching job on his own. We had only been there for a couple of days when he came in and announced that we were moving to Woodward, Oklahoma. I thought, "Boy, he sure is in a good mood. Maybe having his own church will make life better for us all."

We got up early the next morning and headed out for Woodward. We got there in the afternoon. The church was fairly small but nice. The parsonage was right next door to the church and was even nicer than the place we lived at in Hobbs, New Mexico.

Bad Time to Explore

It had two nice bedrooms and a large living room and was furnished with nice furniture. My bed was a full-size bed and I didn't *ever* have a full-size bed. I thought to myself, "Boy, I hope we can stay here for a long time."

We had only been there for a few minutes when some men drove up in a car and J.D. got in with them and drove off.

Mother said to me, "Come on, let's go look at our new church."

As we walked into the front door of the church, the first thing I noticed was that everything was very neat and clean. The church building was old, but everything was well-maintained, not like most of the other churches we had been to, which were usually run-down and dirty. I noticed a plaque on the wall that showed this church had only forty members and it said only twenty-three were present last Sunday.

I didn't remember any of our church homes being this small. I never liked big churches, so I thought this place might be better than the last place.

Mom and I went back to the parsonage and starting unloading everything from the car and trailer. It didn't take long and she told me to go ride my bike and check out the neighborhood while she organized our belongings and put everything up. She said to be back in about an hour and a half in time to eat. I got on my bike and rode down the main part of town, which was only three blocks away from the church. I parked my bike in front of one of the stores and went in to look around. I noticed that everyone was watching me as I looked at the toys. Every time I looked up, I noticed three or four people just looking at me. I thought, "I ain't ever stolen anything in this town or store, so why is everyone watching me?"

It made me nervous, so I made sure I didn't do anything wrong. I just tried to act normal and kept looking at the toys, but every time I looked up, the store clerks were staring at me. I looked up again and saw a man walk over to another clerk as he looked at me, and they began talking as they looked at me. Something was wrong. I tried really hard not to act like I was scared, but I was more frightened than other times when I had actually done something bad. I started walking toward the door, hoping I could get to the front door and get out and jump on my bike before they dreamed up something I did wrong. But that didn't happen, they moved over in front of the door and just stood there as I walked toward them. They stood there staring at me as I got closer and closer to them.

Finally, one of the men asked me, "What is your name?"

I said, "Floyd."

He said, "Where do you live?"

I was too scared to even think clearly, so I just said, "Down that street over there...about three blocks."

He said, "I don't care how many blocks it is to your house, I want to know your address!"

I said, "I don't know it."

He said, "Well, if you don't know where you live, maybe you could tell me how old you are and what grade you are in so I will know what school you should be in right now."

I said, "I ain't started school yet."

He said, "School started three weeks ago, so just tell me the truth. You're skipping school, aren't you?"

I said, "No, I'm not skipping school, I just moved here today!"

He said, "All you kids tell lies when you get caught skipping school."

"But I'm not skipping school!"

"Get in my car, I'm taking you home and talking to your parents," he said, as he grabbed my arm and started walking me down the sidewalk toward his car.

"What about my bike?" I said.

"When you skip school, you take a chance of losing your bike."

He took his hand off of me for a moment to get his car keys out of his pocket and I took off running as hard as I could, picked up my bike and kept running beside it. I put one foot on the pedal and threw my leg over the seat and started peddling as fast as I could. I didn't look back because I was afraid it would slow me down. I rode up to the front yard of our new house and threw my bike down and ran up the steps hollering for Mother. She didn't answer and I turned around, looked out the front door and saw a car pull up and the man from the store got out. I hollered a couple more times for Mother but she didn't answer. Just then she came walking out of the church next door and I ran up to her.

The man asked her, "Is this your son?" and she said, "Yes."

"Why is he not in school?"
Mother said, "We just moved here today a couple of hours ago."

The man introduced himself and said he was the truant officer. He then asked me to come over but I didn't want to get close enough for him to grab me again.

He said, "Come on over, I am not going to grab you again. I know you were telling me the truth now. I've talked with your mother and I am sorry I scared you, but I thought you were skipping school. I hope you like it here. I guess you will be starting school tomorrow?"

I managed to barely say, "Yeah."

He then got in his car and drove off. I went into the house to lie down on my bed. I needed to relax after that scary experience. I lie there thinking this is not a good way to start off in a new place. I hoped it wasn't a sign of bad things to come.

Maybe Not So Stupid

I started school the next day and for the next few weeks, everything was going pretty good. I met a kid, Tommy, at school who had a paper route and I wanted a paper route, too. I think the real reason I wanted it so bad was because I didn't have any money. I wasn't stealing stuff from the stores anymore and I wasn't planning on stealing in this town after what happened with the truant officer. Besides, it was a small town and there weren't many kids to sell stolen toys to anyway. So I had to figure out a way to make some money. My best bet was to make friends with Tommy and learn the paper route business.

Tommy was a serious, quiet kid, like me also small for his age, but unlike me, came from a stable middle-class family. I met his parents later on when they helped me after I'd had a beating from J.D. They were very kind.

After a few weeks of hanging out with Tommy, I decided to make him an offer. I would help him on his paper route for nothing if he would help me get my own route. Tommy said, "It's a deal!" Secretly, I was hoping J.D. would let me help on the paper route. It had been a couple of months since he had hit me and he had only yelled at me a couple of times. Whenever he did yell at me, I would get out of his sight for a while and things would cool down. One thing I had learned was not to ask him for any money, not even lunch money. Mother would save some money out of her grocery money and sneak it to me. But even though things were going better, I didn't look forward to telling J.D. about my paper route plan. I was afraid he was going to want some of the money I planned to make.

At first, I thought to try and catch him in a good mood but realized I didn't know how to catch J.D. in a good mood. You'd think things were going great and then I would ask a question and he went nuts. There was no way to know if this was one of those questions. I decided to face it one day as I rode home on my bike and saw his car in the driveway. I went in the house and J.D. was sitting in his chair listening to the radio. One thing I did know was that you didn't disturb him when he was listening to the radio unless you wanted to be knocked around a bit. I went to my room and laid down, trying to think of the best way to approach him. Once I heard the radio go off, I got up and rushed into the living room to talk with him before he got something else started that I would be interrupting. I tried to think of some plan, but couldn't, so I just blurted it out.

"I got a friend named Tommy who wants me to help him with his paper route."

"What do you mean, help him with his paper route?"

"Well, we will get up at five in the morning and throw papers before school and we do collections after school for a couple of hours."

J.D. said, "What is he going to pay you?"

I said, "Nothing, at first."

J.D. didn't say anything, just had this look on his face that I had seen before whenever he got crazy mad. So I was ready to run if he came out of his chair. He just sat there staring at me for about a minute and said, "If you are stupid enough to work for nothing……go ahead!"

I was so glad he said okay, I didn't care he called me stupid. I started going with Tommy every morning and afternoon. It was worth getting up early to just have more time away from J.D. He was always a gripe in the mornings and many times would cause me to be late to school by giving me a last-minute chore. Sometimes he would have me run to the store on my bike and get him something. It was like he wanted me to be late to school and do poorly, too. Now I got up and left to go on the paper route before he got up and I didn't get home until around six in the evening.

Big Need in a Small Town

Tommy and I would go by the drugstore most every day after making some paper collections and he would buy me a coke and a candy bar for helping him. This was okay for now, but I would rather have my own money.

I would go by the 5 & 10 Cent Store after I had finished collecting with Tommy. I would just walk around looking and trying to think of something that I could sell to the other kids. Pocket knives, pocket radios, and pocket-size flashlights were real hot items. The radios were the most popular and were small enough to fit in my shirt pocket, too. They had an earplug on a cord and a person could get two or three stations with music but a lot of static, too. It was still the coolest thing around.

As I walked through the stores, I noticed it was a lot harder to steal anything in this new town. I always felt like someone was watching me, just like the first day when the truant officer was. So I backed off from stealing and decided to just wait for my paper route to come up.

I had worked with Tommy for a couple of weeks when the paper station manager came over to me and said Tommy told him I would like to have a paper route. I told him I sure would like one. He told me when one opens up, he would give it to me.

Well, after another three weeks, Tommy and I were at the paper station folding papers and the station manager came over to me and asked if I was ready for a route. I said, "Yep, I'm ready!"

He took me to his desk in the back of the station and began to explain what he expected of me. "You have to keep track of all your collections."

Well, I already knew all about collecting, because I had been helping Tommy for over a month. Then he began to tell me that my route had thirty-five customers and I would get thirty-five papers every morning at the station. I would have to pay for all the papers every Friday at a cost of three cents each, which meant I would have to pay $7.35 every Friday. He also told me the reason I got the route was because he had to let the other boy go because he wasn't paying for his papers every Friday. My job was to make all collections so I would have the money to pay him every Friday. Then he explained that if I made all thirty-five of my collections at five cents each then, I would have collected $12.25. So after I paid him...I would make $4.90 a week. He also told me that there were one hundred thirty-one houses on my route and if I did some door-to-door selling of new subscriptions to the daily paper, I could make even more money and easily double my income.

I thought, "Boy if I work hard, I could even make $10.00 a week."

My first week went pretty good and I had added a couple of new customers. The manager said I was doing a good job. I did well on my paper route all winter and spring.

It was about a month and a half before school would be out and I wasn't sure if I was ready for that. It meant more time with J.D. The last summer was the worst summer of my life. Luckily, things had not been as bad since we had moved to Woodward. I still got knocked around about once a month but usually, it was only two or three hits. There were a few times he did beat me up pretty bad. He would only yell at me in front of Mother and there were a few times he hit me in front of her. When he did that, they always had a big argument and I would just leave the house. I hoped if I wasn't around, things might settle down. I was tired of all these arguments about me.

I wished I could just go live with my Grandma and Uncle George, but I had no way to get to Oklahoma City. I would just say to myself: "This is just the way it has to be...I just have to live with it."

Surprise Attack

Summer was coming up and I was going to try and make the best of it. Every morning after Tommy and me finished throwing our papers, we would meet up and go to school together. After school, we would do our collections together. One evening after we finished up, I headed home on my bike. I walked into the back door and into the kitchen. J.D. was standing at the kitchen sink looking out the window. I walked over to the cabinet to get me a glass so I could get some water. As I reached for the cabinet door, he turned around and hit me, knocking me all the way across the kitchen. It totally took me by surprise and I was stunned for a moment. I tried to get up, but he was already over me, hitting me again before I could do anything. I just curled up on the floor in the corner while he continued to hit me.

As he hit me, he was yelling at me about something, but I never understood what he was mad about after he quit hitting me. I just lay there for a few moments and after I knew he was gone, I managed to sit up and lean back on the wall. I hurt all over so I just sat by the wall for a while longer. When I tried to get up, I felt this sharp pain in my side and I could hardly move, the pain was so bad. I couldn't get up so I just crawled to my room. After several attempts, I managed to get on my bed. I wondered where Mom was and part of me wished she was there to help me while another part of me was glad she didn't witness what had happened. As I lay on the bed, I began to try to think of some way to get back at J.D.

I heard someone come in the front door and hoped it was Mom, as I didn't think I could survive any more beating from J.D. I heard her voice and it was a big relief. But I didn't want her to see me hurt like this, so I covered up my body and head, pretending to be asleep as she opened my door to look in on me. I lay awake in bed because of the pain most of the night.

The next morning I was supposed to throw my paper route, but there was no way I could do it. I also didn't want to just lie in bed all day, because Mom would come in and figure out something was wrong. I managed to get up. I didn't have to dress because I slept in my clothes. I could barely walk, but I managed to go into the kitchen and grab some cookies Mom had made the day before, put some in a sack, get a quart of milk from the icebox and head outside. It was still early and dark outside, but it was always dark when I left for my paper route on regular mornings. I started to get on my bike but hurt too much, so I just pushed it. I wasn't paying much attention to where I was going, I just thought how much I would love to get away from all of this. I would like to just run away, but where would I go? How would I get there? I even thought maybe I could just get a big club and sneak up on J.D. and hit him. But if I didn't hit him hard enough to hurt him really bad or knock him out, I just might make him mad enough to kill me.

No Place to Hide

It was almost daylight and when I looked up, I saw I had walked to school. I was thinking about what happened so much that I didn't even think about where I was going. I pushed my bike onto the schoolyard and leaned it against a tree in order to finish eating my cookies and drink my milk. The sun was coming up quickly and I didn't know what it was but I knew I had to think something up fast. *"What am I going to do today? I can't go to school all beat up. I can't hang out in town. I need to find a place not too far away because I just don't feel like going very far."*

I remembered a pond just outside of town about eight blocks from the school. It was right next to the road and the dam on the pond was high enough for me to hide out because you couldn't see me from the road. I started walking and pushing my bike and by now the sun was shining brightly and I saw more cars move around on all the streets. I didn't want anyone to see, so I managed to get on my bike so I could get there faster. I got to the pond and there was a fence between the road and the dam. I thought, *"There ain't no way I can get my bike over this fence and I can't leave it beside the road."* So I just decided I had to go somewhere else. I couldn't chance going back through the town, so I just kept riding my bike right out of town.

I kept riding until the paved road turned into a dirt road. As I headed out into the country, I hoped I would see a place where I could stay for the day. I was also worried that a school bus might come by me any minute, too. Finally, I came to a gate in the fence and it only had a wire looped over the post to keep it closed. I unhooked the gate and pushed my bike in as fast as I could, hoping no one would drive by and see me. I hooked the gate back and headed back to the dam. I lay my bike down on the side of the dam and lay down by a tree. It felt good to finally be able to relax with the sun beating down on my face. I was so tired that I fell asleep.

When I woke up, the first thing I noticed was the sun was on the other side of the earth, so I knew it had to be later in the afternoon. I wasn't sure school was out but thought it was, so I got my bike and headed back to town. As I was riding through town, a car pulled up beside me, and it was Tommy. He stuck his head out of the window and said, "Hey, what are you doing?"

Before I could answer, he said, "What happened to your face? Mom, look at his face, it looks like someone beat him up!"

I responded abruptly, "No, no one beat me up...I crashed on my bike!"

Tommy said, "Hey, you don't have to get mad."

I said, "I'm sorry, I don't mean to sound mad."

His mom said, "Did your parents take you to a doctor?"

I said, "No."

"You mean your mom didn't think you need to see a doctor?"

I said, "No."

"Well, how about your dad?"

I said, "He looked at it and said it didn't look too bad."

She said, "I think it looks really bad so we are going to follow you home to your house and get your mom to take you to a doctor that we know that is really good."

I said, "My parents went to a church meeting today and won't be home until late tonight."

She just looked at me for a moment like she knew I was lying and then she said, "Okay, why don't you follow us on your bike over to our house, and I will take a look at you."

I said, "Okay."

As I started to take off on my bike, a sharp pain went through my side and I would have fallen except Tommy's dad jumped out of the car and caught me. He told Tommy to get my bike and ride to their house while he carried me and put me in their car.

I said, "Okay if you promise to not take me home or to a doctor." Tommy's dad and mom looked at me for a moment, then looked at each other, then said, "Okay."

Tommy's dad helped me into the car. Everyone was very quiet during the ride to their house. When we got there, I went in and sit on their sofa. Tommy's mom and dad sat across the room from me, and his mom started asking me questions.

She said, "I guess you must have fallen off your bike on your way home after helping Tommy on this paper route."

I said, "Yes Ma'am."

"And your mother wasn't at home when you got there?"

"No. I just went to bed because I didn't feel good."

She said, "Well, what about this morning? Didn't your mom wonder why you were staying home from school?"

Each time she asked another question, it got harder to come up with answers. When I agreed to come to Tommy's house, I didn't know I was going to get the third-degree interrogation. Each time she asked a question, I would have to pause a little longer to think up a new answer. She just sat there looking at me, waiting for each answer.

After a while, I said, "When my mom came to get me out of bed, I told her I didn't feel good enough to go to school."

She asked, "You mean your mom didn't check on you or ask you what was wrong? She didn't even check to see if you had a fever?"

"No."

I sat there for a moment, thinking I really needed to leave before she asked me any more questions. I said, "I guess I better go home now."

She said, "I want you to stay and eat dinner with us first. Besides, you already told us that your parents aren't going to be home until late. I won't ask you any more questions if you stay...okay?"

I said, "Okay."

She also told me she would like for me to come by tomorrow after school when Tommy and I were finished with our paper route. She said, "I want to see how well you are doing. I'm worried about that pain in your side. You know you could have some broken ribs."

She paused for a minute and said, "I don't see how you could crash so bad on your bike to get so beat up."

Tommy said, "I have seen him several times before like this after he crashed on his bike."

His mom said, "Have you ever seen him have one of these bad crashes?"

"Well, no...but I usually see him right after or the next day. One time I saw him and his face looked worse than it does now!"

Tommy's mom said, "Well, I'm going to get dinner on the table, you boys just stay here in the living room and visit until it is ready."

Tommy's dad went into the kitchen to help her with dinner. Tommy told me he wished I would come by more often because he was the one who usually had to go help in the kitchen. He was still talking to me, but I was trying to listen to what his mom was saying to his dad in the kitchen. I heard her say that she didn't think I fell off my bike and thinks someone is beating me up. She continued to tell his dad that they needed to find out what is really happening to me. I didn't want them to do anything because I was afraid of what might happen if they said anything to J.D.

We went in to eat dinner and I only ate a little bit and then I told them I really needed to go home. His dad offered to take me home and let Tommy ride my bike home for me. I refused the offer and told them I felt well enough to ride my bike home. When I went out to get on my bike, Tommy followed me out and whispered to me that he did my paper route for me that morning and also told me he would do it for me tomorrow morning if I didn't feel good enough. I told him I thought I could make it tomorrow. I asked him what the paper manager said about me not showing up. Tommy said, "He just wanted to know where you were and I told him you probably just overslept. I told him I would do your route for you."

Tommy said if I didn't make it tomorrow, he would tell the manager I got hurt. As I rode off, I told Tommy I would be there tomorrow morning. By now it was almost dark and the time I usually get home after making my collections. At least I wouldn't have to deal with J.D. because after a good beating, he always laid off of me for a couple days. So I could just go home and go to bed and get a good night's sleep.

After a few days, my bruises began to heal up and I was kind of back to normal. I never heard anything more from Tommy's parents and I sure was glad, because it would only have made matters worse. Tommy would ask me to come over for dinner and I would make up excuses. I was hoping if his parents didn't see me, then maybe they would forget the incident.

Summer came and went very fast and school was starting. I didn't like school, but it was better than being at home and being J.D.'s slave all day. I was so far behind in school that I didn't think I could ever catch up. The time I spent in the little church school where they didn't teach me anything, plus moving all the time, had caused me to get way behind on my basics. Plus, I just lost interest.

Sometimes I wished we were back on the move again and changing schools every three or four weeks. Then I wouldn't have to care what a teacher thought about me. If a teacher thought I was dumb, it was no big deal if I was moving in a few weeks. But being in the same school for a year or more, I found myself beginning to care about what the teachers thought of me. I didn't like being thought of as a dummy!

Money, Money, Who Has the Money?

A couple of weeks after school started, my guardian angel made my wish come true. J.D. had been talking to a farmer about joining the church. This farmer was well-off and had been coming to church for four or five Sundays. I remember one Saturday evening what a good mood J.D. was in. I hadn't seen him like this since he and Mom got married. He was telling Mom that this farmer was going to join the church Sunday morning and that it was going to be a good thing for the church. The next morning he was still in a good mood and all J.D. could talk about was what a good man this farmer was and he would be glad to have him in the church during the morning service.

Sunday morning the farmer joined the church, and after the church service, he and J.D. went somewhere for the rest of the afternoon. It was unusual for J.D. to go anywhere on a Sunday afternoon, as he usually would sit around and just think of things for me to do for him. He came home right before the evening church service. The only thing he said to me was that he wanted me to come straight home right after school on Monday. He said I couldn't do any paper route collections and that it was very important that I come straight home. I was surprised that he didn't yell at me or give me a bunch of chores to do that afternoon. He also told me I didn't have to go to evening church service. That made me happy. I didn't know what came over him, he was in such a great mood. He had never been this nice to me.

After school on Monday, I told Tommy I had to go straight home and couldn't go make collections. He was disappointed but as he rode off on his bike, he shouted, "See you tomorrow!" I didn't know that this would be the last time I would ever see my friend Tommy.

When I got home, I walked into the house and saw boxes stacked up in the living room and kitchen. I asked Mom what was going on and J.D. said, "Don't ask questions, and just help your mother."

I went into my bedroom where Mom was packing my clothes. I didn't say anything because I knew J.D. could hear. We were moving again. We continued packing until after dark, all this time nobody saying anything. Mom and J.D. were not talking. I was wondering what happened today that could be so bad that we had to move. Why, just yesterday, J.D. was so happy and in such a good mood. I didn't dare ask a question, instead, I kept packing.

About an hour after dark, J.D. told me to come with him and help him hook up the trailer behind the car. He backed the trailer up to the front porch and we started loading everything into the trailer. It didn't take us very long because J.D was throwing things in the trailer as fast as he could. I didn't know what was up and I wasn't very surprised because leaving in the middle of the night was normal for us. I was just mad. This was the first time in a long time we had stayed long enough for me to make some real friends and actually begin to like school.

When we drove off, I knew I would never see Tommy again. I was eleven years old and thought I was too old to be crying, but I couldn't help it. I wondered if I was going to ever have a life like other kids as I sat in the back seat surrounded by clothes and boxes. My eyes began to tear up but I just gritted my teeth to keep from making a sound. I finally went to sleep and was woken up by Mom telling me to come into the motel.

I said, "Where are we?" and she said, "We are in Oklahoma City."

The next morning, J.D. woke me up, telling me to get dressed because we were going to go eat breakfast. He was nice to me for a change, but I wondered what was really going on. Usually, when we left somewhere in the middle of the night, J.D. was mad for days. When we returned from breakfast, he told me to get all the boxes and clothes out of the car, even stuff in the glove box and underneath the car seats. After I finished, he told Mom he had some business to take care of and that he would be back after lunch. He gave Mom some money for us to eat lunch on and told her where a cafe was down the street that we could walk to. I helped him unhook the trailer and he drove off.

I unloaded my bike from the trailer and just rode around most of the morning. Then Mom and I went to lunch. I tried to get Mom to tell me what was going on but she just said, "I don't want to talk about it." Later that afternoon, J.D. came home driving a brand new 1949 Ford. It was black and shiny and I thought it was the best looking car I had ever seen. We got into the car and took a ride. J.D. started to tell us that he had another church in Altus, Oklahoma that needed a new minister. He and Mom were in such a good mood, that I thought maybe with a new car and new church, our life would be better. Maybe we could be a happy family after all.

I didn't think about where the money came from to buy the new car. I was just enjoying everyone being in a good mood and the luxury of having a new car! Later on in my life, Mother told me that the farmer who joined the church in Woodward had given several thousand dollars in tithes when he joined because he had a great crop that year. J.D. justified taking the money, telling Mom that he had not been paid what he was promised, so when the money came in, he took it for his own back pay. She went along with him at the time but told me that she knew down deep that it was wrong.

We stayed in the motel a couple more days before we headed to Altus. When we pulled up to our new church home, I asked, "Is this it?" J.D. didn't like my tone of voice and snapped at me, "What the hell is wrong with this church?"

I said, "Nothing, I just expected it to be a bigger church."

We were only there a few minutes when some church members came to greet us. They helped us unload our belongings into the little house by the church. This house was small and dumpy and not nearly as nice as the one we had in Woodward. After we unloaded everything, I went riding on my bike to check out the town. I rode by the school to see where it was because I knew I would be starting the next day.

I didn't like the school in Altus from the beginning. I didn't get along with the teachers or the other kids. I became a loner and would cut school a lot. Of course, when I cut school, I would usually go to the movies or go out to the air force base and watch the planes take off and land. I did manage to get me a paper route and that gave me a little spending money. Every once in a while J.D. would still bang me around and I would have to go to school all bruised up and tell my teachers that I crashed on my bike or that I got into a fight.

I think I had developed a bad attitude because I wasn't liked by any of the kids or teachers. I also developed another problem at home—bed wetting. I don't know why I just couldn't wake up when I needed to go. Sometimes I would just sit up until two or three in the morning, going to the bathroom numerous times in hopes that when I went to sleep I wouldn't wet the bed. I would still wake up the next morning all wet. I tried to hide this from J.D. because I knew he would beat me.

Mother helped me hide it by getting all my bedding and washing it before J.D. could see it. One time he came in my room early in the morning when I was still asleep and jerked all my covers off and grabbed my arm, pulled me out of bed and slammed me against the wall. When my head hit the wall I thought I was going to pass out and I wish I could pass out so I couldn't feel J.D. punching me with his fist. He beat me up really bad this time. I guess he did this because I wet the bed. I managed to get up after he left and go into the bathroom and wash off all the blood because I didn't want my mom to see me in this condition. When I went back into the bedroom, I saw blood on the wall and on the floor so I got a rag and wiped it up.

Then I went out on the porch swing for a minute to think about what I wanted to do because I wasn't going to school in this shape. I couldn't stay at home either, so I just got on my bike and started riding. It wasn't daylight yet, so I thought I would go out to the air force base and watch the planes land in the dark. I had only been there a few minutes when I remembered I was supposed to throw papers today. But I realized I physically couldn't do it. They would have to just do without me today. I sat down on the grass and leaned back on a fence post and watched the planes come and go. I fell asleep sitting there and when I woke up, the sun was shining down on me. I felt like I was cooking in the sun but the sun seemed to make my bruises feel better.

Finally, I got up and rode my bike over to the park. There I found a nice shade tree to sit under and as I sat there, I told myself I had to find a way out of this mess. I thought that maybe I could steal a gun and follow J.D. when he left the house and shoot him. But what if I got caught? I would go to jail forever! Then I remembered this man that went to our church who had a heart attack and died. I wished J.D. would have a heart attack and die, too. Then Mom and I could go back to just taking care of each other.

Escape Plan

As the days went by, my only thought was how to get away from J.D. I came up with the idea of running away. So I began to plan my escape. I would run away to Oklahoma City where my grandmother and Uncle George lived.

I decided for sure to go and stay with them, but I didn't know how I would get there. Maybe I could hitchhike or just save up money and ride my bike. I really wanted my bike with me, so I decided that the only way I could escape would be on my bike. For the last few years, my bike had been my only means of escape and I didn't feel like I could do without it. So I made up my mind to ride my bike to Oklahoma City. I figured it would take me all day to ride there. I rode around town a lot already and believed I was capable of riding my bike all day. If I got tired, I would just stop and rest for a while.

I started asking people in town how far Oklahoma City was from Altus. Most everyone said it was about one hundred and fifty miles. I estimated that I could go fifteen miles-per-hour and it would take me ten hours to ride my bike to Oklahoma City. I thought that it would be easy.

So I started planning my trip. I knew I needed to be a long way from the house when J.D. and Mom discovered I was gone. I usually left around 5 a.m. to do my paper route and go to school and did collections after school before arriving home around 8 p.m. This gave me about fifteen hours before they would start looking for me. It took me two weeks and a lot of thinking to come up with this plan. After deciding this was the best way to go, I needed to figure out how much money I needed for my trip. I might have to stop one night somewhere on the way and would need enough money for a motel.

I had stayed in motels with J.D. and Mother in the past and knew the cost ran about $5.00 per night. My food for the trip would probably cost me another $5.00. I made about $3.00 a week on my paper route, so at this rate, it was going to take me three to four weeks to save up enough money. That was if I didn't spend any money at all. No movies, no candy, no nothing! Just saving all I could. I hoped I could manage to get through the next four weeks without another bad beating. So I spent the next three weeks trying to make J.D. as happy as possible. I saved every penny and came up with twelve dollars in just three weeks. I had lucked out and got by without any beatings.

The time had come for me to pick a day to leave. It was Wednesday and I did most of my collections on Friday and Monday. If I stayed until Monday and left Tuesday morning, I would have more money, but I was taking a chance of J.D. getting mad and beating the hell out of me and I would not be physically able to leave. So I decided to leave Friday morning. I didn't even want to go to school on Thursday but decided to anyway because I didn't want the truant officer coming by the house and talking to Mom or J.D.

Putting the Plan in Action

After school on Thursday, I started preparing my bike for the trip. I oiled and adjusted the chain and checked all my nuts and bolts to make sure they were tight. I rode down to the gas station and checked the air pressure in my tires. I hurried back to the house because I didn't want to make J.D. mad for going somewhere without his permission. I stayed out of his sight as much as possible, hoping and praying that nothing would go wrong. If I got a beating, I didn't think I would be able to make the trip. The day of the trip I woke up early around 4 a.m. and at first I thought about how happy I was that I made it to this point without a beating, but as I lay there thinking, I began to get scared about the trip. This was going to be a long trip and I would be all by myself. I had never ridden my bike more than a few miles out of town. I thought I knew the way, but what if I get lost?

I sat up in bed and told myself that I couldn't think about this anymore. I just had to get up and go! Besides, getting lost is better than putting up with J.D. I got out of bed and started putting on my clothes very quietly. I didn't take any extra clothes with me because I didn't want the extra weight. I grabbed my paper bag, threw it over the handlebars of my bike and started riding away. I had a map in my paper bag that I had gotten from a filling station. I had marked the roads I needed to take to Oklahoma City. It was still dark outside when I reached the edge of town. I tried not to think about what I was doing because when I did, it made me feel scared. So I just rode along trying to think about what I was going to do when I got to Oklahoma City. When the sun came out, most of my fear had left me. I began to enjoy riding along the countryside. After I had ridden quite awhile, I saw a gas station coming up down the road. I decided to stop and buy myself a coke and candy bar. I only stopped long enough to drink my coke and eat my candy bar, because I needed to keep moving. It wasn't very long before I came to my first town. I saw a cafe on the side of the road and realized I was hungry. I stopped and had some breakfast. The clock on the wall said 9:15 a.m. and I checked my map to see where I was and I guessed that it was Lawton, Oklahoma. I didn't dare ask anyone for fear that I might be discovered as a runaway.

When I was at home I just ate cereal and milk for breakfast, but I noticed everyone in the cafe was eating a big breakfast. I ordered eggs and ham and a big glass of milk. When I went to leave and pay, it cost me sixty-five cents. Wow, I hoped that I didn't have to pay that much for my hamburger at lunch time. As I rode through the town, I saw a lot of places that I would like to stop and visit, but I knew I had to keep on moving. I checked my map to make sure I was still on the right road. It was almost 9:30 a.m. when I left the restaurant, which meant I had been on the road about four hours. I was not getting tired yet, probably because I had been riding at a slow, steady pace. I began to worry about making it in one day. I worried if I would have enough money to stay in a motel, so I decided to pick up the pace a little bit. I tried this for a few miles and my legs got so tired that I had to stop for a rest. I decided to go back to my slow, steady pace. I just might have to sleep in a park or somewhere beside the road if I didn't make it in one day.

I rode for another hour or so and came to another little town. I saw a Dairy Queen and by the position of the sun, I guessed it was about noon. I stopped and got me a burger. I checked my map and saw I was about half-way to Oklahoma City. My next town on the map was Chickasha, about thirty miles away. I got back to peddling and when I got to Chickasha, I rode by a couple schools. Students were still in school, so I knew it wasn't three o'clock yet. I was making pretty good time. I stopped and got myself another candy bar and coke at a gas station. I didn't want to waste time so I ate and drank fast so I could hurry back on the road. By now, I figured I had about fifty miles to go and it was around 2 p.m. If I rode hard, I could probably be there by 7 p.m. I was getting tired, but I didn't want to spend the night on the road. I knew I would have to push hard to get there today.

Explaining Harder Than Pedaling

I rode up in front of Grandma's house just before dark. I didn't go inside for a few minutes. I didn't know what I was going to say to her. I got off my bike and went up and sat down on the front porch. Grandma opened the front door and saw me sitting there. She looked really surprised and it took her a while to say something.

"Honey, whut ya doing here?" She looked all around and asked, "How did ya git here? Whar is yer mom an' J.D.?"

I froze for a few minutes, not saying anything. I looked at her and said, "I came by myself."

By this time Uncle George had stepped out on the porch, too, and said, "Ya come by yerself? Come on in this house an' sit down an' tell me whut's wrong."

I went in the house, sit down, and told them I just couldn't live with J.D. anymore. Grandma asked, "Has J.D. been mean t' ya?" I just sat there and didn't answer her. Everyone was quiet for several minutes. I guess nobody knew what to say.

After a bit, Uncle George asked, "How did ya git here?"

"I rode my bike."

He said, "Nobody can ride a bike that fer!"

"I did."

He said, "Whar is yer bike?"

I showed him it was over on the front porch. I could tell he was having a hard time believing me but he didn't say anything else about it. Grandma said, "Ya must be hungry, come in th' kitchen an' I'll fix ya something t'eat."

While Grandma was fixing food, Uncle George went out and got my bike and put it on the porch. After I had eaten, I had settled down and started telling them how I had planned my trip for a long time. I told them all about my trip and how long it took me. I also told them how Mom would not be missing me until about now because of my collecting on my paper route.

Grandma said, "Yeah, but she'll be worrying by morning, so we better call her an' let her know ya is alright."

"Grandma, I'm too tired to talk…I just want to go to bed."

Grandma said, "Okay, I'll call an' talk with yer mom."

I was really tired but I still had a lot going on in my mind when I went to bed. I wasn't sure what I did was right or wrong. I couldn't go to sleep. I just lay there wondering what was going to happen tomorrow. Part of me wanted to just cry, but I knew that wouldn't do any good. I didn't get much sleep that night, mainly because I was worried about what would happen tomorrow and what J.D. might do. I was only twelve years old and in my mind, I thought he might do something bad to Grandma and Uncle George. Maybe that is the reason I didn't tell them he beat me. Did my coming here put them in danger? What if he came here tomorrow and went crazy on them like he did with me?

I started to leave in the middle of the night, but the more I thought about it, I was afraid he would be madder if I was not here and might accuse Grandma and Uncle George of hiding me. That would really make him mad. I finally went to sleep and when I woke up the next morning, Grandma told me she had called Mom and they were coming to get me. Now I was thinking I made a big mistake because J.D. was not going to like this at all. After breakfast, Grandma and Uncle George began to ask me more questions about why I ran away. I didn't know what to tell them because I was afraid to tell them what J.D. had been doing to me since he married Mom. Part of me was afraid they might not believe me, too. I didn't know what to say so I sat in silence.

Uncle George said, "Boy, whut's wrong? Thar has t'be a reason why ya come here."

Searching for a Way Out

I had to say something, so I told Grandma and Uncle George that I was having trouble at school and would like to stay with them. They said it would be okay if my mother agreed. That made me feel a lot better because I thought Mom would let me stay. As the day wore on while we waited for Mom and J.D., I felt pretty sure that I would stay and that my bicycle trip had been worthwhile.

Mother and J.D. arrived in the late afternoon. As they got out of the car, something came over me—for some reason, I didn't want to go hug my mom. I just stood there looking at her. As they walked to the porch, Mother gave me a hug and asked me what was wrong? Again I didn't say anything. Then J.D. tried to give me a hug, but I stepped away quickly and gave him a look like I would like to kill him. Even today, when I close my eyes and see him standing there trying to look like *Mr. Religious Holy Man*, I get mad!

When Grandma said that supper was ready and called us in to eat, I didn't go in. Instead, I got on my bike, rode to the park and sit for awhile until it began to get dark.

When I went back, J.D. asked me where I had been. I didn't answer. I walked to the bedroom and started getting ready for bed. Mother came in and asked what was wrong. I had never acted like this toward her, but something came over me when I saw J.D. I didn't even understand why I was acting like this. Loudly snapping at my mother, I said nothing was wrong. I just wanted to go to bed and be left alone. I got what I wanted. Nobody bothered me the rest of the night, but I didn't sleep much.

The next morning, the first thing I heard was to hurry up and eat my breakfast so we could go home. I realized that J.D. had convinced Mother to not let me stay with Grandma and Uncle George. I told Mother that I didn't need anything to eat so we could just go.

Once outside, I started pushing my bike toward the car and J.D. said, "You're not taking that thing!"

I said, "I'm taking my bike or I ain't going and you can't make me. If you try, I'll take off down the railroad track and you will never see me again."

My grandmother lived next to the track that led into a wooded area where a lot of hobos lived. I knew I could hide and they would not be able to find me. J.D. agreed to take the bike. All I could think about on the way home was how I was going to deal with him. I knew it was not going to be good. At this point, I was pretty much over my fear and was just mad. I didn't care how anyone felt or if my mother would be mad if I did something to J.D. I thought of killing him or breaking both his legs—the latter being harder than the former—but if I did either, I would be in trouble for a long time. I thought I could hide out. I had heard of people changing their names. Maybe I could, too, but worried about what would happen to me if I didn't get away with it. Would it be worth the risk?

I thought about running away again—but to a different place. A friend of mine I had barely met in Oklahoma City just before my mother married J.D. had moved to Dallas about a year earlier and we had kept in touch. His name was Eugene, he was tall with red hair and freckles, and was very respectful to his parents and all adults. He was a really nice boy, not a fighter like me. We became close friends soon after I clipped the notebook on the smart-aleck kid's ear. He didn't like that boy, either. When J.D. came on the scene and Eugene knew we were leaving town, he asked me to write him with my new address, which I did each time I moved.

Between the ages of eight, when we first met, and twelve, he would write me every two or three months—long letters about his school, family, and life. I wrote him and told him about J.D. beating me up. When the mail arrived wherever we lived, when I was expecting a letter from Eugene, I would get to the mailbox before J.D. I was afraid Eugene would say something about the beatings in his letters and didn't want J.D. to read it. I always kept an envelope with his address on it but tore up the letters. I thought I had an envelope at home with his address. He had the family life I wished for—loving parents and a stable home life. Maybe I could stay with them for a while.

Kill or Run

The rest of the way home, I went over all of the possibilities, but couldn't decide whether I wanted to kill J.D. or run away. When we finally got home, I was exhausted from thinking. At least it kept me from thinking about what J.D. was going to do to me. As we walked in, J.D. said, "I guess you know I owe you one for all the trouble you caused and the worry you put your mother through by running away."

Saying nothing, I went to my bedroom, shut the door, layed down and kicked off my shoes. My mind was too tired from trying to plan what to do next. I must have fallen asleep. When I woke up, I remembered that Charlie, my paper route friend, didn't know what happened to me. I needed to think up something to tell him about why I had missed throwing my paper route.

J.D. came in and told me to come home after school because he had some things to get straight with me. No way was I coming straight home after school because I needed to throw my papers. Besides, coming home would make no difference. J.D. would still beat the hell out of me the first time Mother was not around to see him do it.

During the next week, I was not home unless Mother was there. Then, on Saturday morning, J.D. came into my bedroom, pulled me out of bed and started beating me. I don't remember what happened over the next few days. The next thing I remember was hearing my friend Charlie at the front door, asking J.D. where I was. J.D. told him that I was on a trip with my mom and would be back in a few days. I was afraid that he had done something to my mom. I had to get out of the house. I had on bloody clothes but I hurt too much to change them.

Slipping out the back door, I saw that it was almost dark. Because of my pain, I couldn't ride my bike but pushed it down the alley, looking back to be sure that J.D. hadn't seen me. As soon as I was sure that no one could see me from the house, I wondered where I was going. I didn't know anyone except Charlie. As soon as I reached the park, I sat down for a few minutes but didn't stay long, because J.D. might be driving around looking for me.

Port in the Storm

I decided to go to Charlie's house. I took all the alleys to get there and parked my bike in the backyard out of sight. What was I going to tell them? I had never told anyone but Eugene that J.D. beat me. If I did, would they go to the police? What would happen to my mom? Now she was missing and I didn't know what had happened to her. I didn't know what to do, but I knew I had to do something. I knocked, but when the door opened I couldn't say anything. I just stood there looking at Charlie's dad. He said, "What happened to you, boy? Come in this house and let me look at you."

I went in and he yelled for Charlie's mom to come. She came running from the back of the house. When she saw me, she stopped in shock for a minute then looked me over and asked where I hurt. I told her that I hurt all over. She said, "We have got to get this boy to a hospital!"

"No!" I said. "I can't go to the hospital!"

She asked why. Then Charlie told her that he had been at my house this morning and had been told by my dad that my mom and I were out of town for a few days. "Why did your dad say that?"

I said, "I need to go, I shouldn't have come here."

Charlie's mom said I wasn't going anywhere.

I said, "Please don't take me to the hospital or to the police station."

"Why would we want to take you to a police station? Have you done something bad?"

Then Charlie spoke up again and said that I hadn't been to school for a while and hadn't been helping on the paper route. "I've taken care of your route for three days."

"I helped you yesterday."

"No, you didn't. You ain't helped me since Friday."

He and his mom looked at me for what seemed like minutes.

"Today is Tuesday," his mom said. I was confused now.

"What day do you think it is?" she asked.

"Saturday."

"You mean you don't remember Saturday, Sunday, Monday, and part of today?"

I didn't say anything.

"Let's clean you up," she said, "and see how bad you're hurt. You can wear some of Charlie's clothes and then we will figure out what to do."

She wiped off most of the blood and looked at all my bruises but decided I didn't have any broken bones. Then she sent me to the bathroom to wash up and put on Charlie's clothes. When I came out, she asked me if I was hungry. She had some warm soup for me to eat and after I finished, we would have me checked for internal injuries at the hospital.

I said, "NO! You can't take me to the hospital and don't ask me why. I can't tell you!"

She said, "Okay. Calm down. Everything is going to be okay. Where is your mom? Your dad said she was with you."

I just sat there saying nothing and I'm sure I had a very upset look on my face because his mom kept saying, "Everything is going to be okay."

They decided not to take me to the hospital that night, but I knew they would have to do something with me the next day, so I had to think of what to do. I decided to sneak out of the house after everyone had gone to sleep, but I fell asleep and woke up as the sun was coming up. Everyone was still asleep, so I managed to sneak out. Getting some rest made me feel better— even good enough to ride my bike if I rode slowly. I went to the park and hid in a dark area where trees hid me from the road. I sat down by a tree trunk and fell asleep again. When I awoke, the sun was shining brightly.

What I needed was to find Mom. I rode toward the house, trying to think of a way to check things out and not get caught by J.D. Then I remembered an old building across the street from our house and down the alley. I rode by it and noticed a door ajar and nothing inside. I was able to put my bike inside and leave the door open just enough to see when J.D. backed his car out of the driveway. When he left, I planned to go in the house and see if I could find any clue as to what happened to Mom.

I sat there waiting and watching for what seemed like hours. I don't know how much time passed before I saw the front door open and out comes Mother sweeping off the front porch. She looked fine and I was relieved—but also confused. Where had she been? I was just realizing that today was Tuesday and wondering where I had been for the last few days. I felt like I was going crazy. I didn't know what to do. I sat down and tried to think about everything going on. When I looked up, I saw a police car pull up in front of my house. I knew that Charlie's parents had called the police, but I had no intention of going home again. I had to run away to a place where no one could find me. What was I going to do? My mind was too twisted to think straight. If I had a place where I could hide and not worry about someone finding me, maybe I could think. Not only was J.D. looking for me, but also the police.

I fell asleep sitting on the floor. When I woke up, it was almost dark, and I was about to look for a new hiding place when I saw Charlie. He was riding his bike up and down in front of my house. I threw a rock at him. He saw me and came over to the little building. I told him to hurry inside before someone saw him.

He said that the police were looking for me and that his mom and dad had told the police that J.D. had beat me and I would be protected if I went to the police station.

I said, "No! No one will believe me. J.D. is a preacher and always convinces everyone that I'm bad, fighting all the time and being bruised. I'm afraid to go to the police. You have to help me do something."

Waiting It Out

We stood there staring at each other for a few seconds. Charlie said, "I know an old warehouse down by the railroad track that nobody has used it for a long time. You could stay there for a few days and I will bring you some food."

We waited until after dark before heading down there. The warehouse was in an old part of town where most of the buildings were abandoned. One of the doors of the warehouse was open and we entered.

Charlie said, "I have to get home and can't come back tonight. Hope you are not too hungry until I bring you something to eat in the morning before I go to school."

After he left, I realized how hungry I really was but I knew I had to make it until morning. The building that I was staying in was very dark. There were a couple of floodlights not too far away so I had a little light. I set my bike over by the door so if anyone came through the door, it would knock my bike over. I just sat down on the floor wondering what I was going to do. I knew that I was going to run away again, but now I had no time to plan like last time.

No Time for Goodbyes

The next morning Charlie brought me a sandwich and had to hurry off to school. As I said good-bye, I thought maybe I would not see him again because I knew I could not stay here any longer. I sat there thinking about what I was going to do...then it hit me. I needed to go back to my house and get the letter from my friend Eugene so I would have his address in Dallas. I knew I had to be very careful because if I got caught skipping school by the truant officer, he would take me to my mom and J.D.

I got on my bike and started to head toward my house, staying in the alleyways and hoping no one saw me. I had to be very careful because I was skipping school. As I rode in the alley, I drove behind a gas station and realized I was thirsty and decided to go inside and put a nickel in the coke machine and get a coke. The station manager was outside talking to a customer and hadn't seen me go inside. So I went over to the cash register and opened it. When it opened, a bell rang loudly which really scared me. Luckily the station manager didn't hear the bell, so I grabbed three twenty-dollar bills and ran out of the station, got on my bike and rode away as fast as I could.

Now I had some money to run away from home. I rode my bike to the little building down the alley from my house so I could see when J.D. and Mother left. After a short time, I saw them get into the car and drive off. I hurried to my house, parked my bike in the back and went inside to look for the letter from Eugene. After I found it, I hurried into the kitchen and grabbed some bread, lunchmeat, and a quart of milk. I put it all in a paper bag and rode off on my bike as fast as I could back to the old warehouse. I sat down to eat and tried to think of what to do next.

I remembered a truck stop down by the railroad tracks three blocks away. Maybe I could hitch a ride with a truck driver that was heading for Dallas. I waited in the warehouse until time for school to be out so I didn't draw any attention to myself for skipping school. I rode over to the truck stop and went inside and sat down at the counter. I told the waitress I wanted a hamburger and a coke. She said, "Do you have any money?"

I said, "Yeah," and pulled out one of my twenty-dollar bills.

She said, "Where did you get all that money?"

Her question caught me off-guard and I had to think quick.

I said, "My grandma gave it to me to get back home."

She asked, "Where is your home?"

I answered, "Dallas."

She said, "Dallas! Why don't your parents pick you up or your grandmother take you home?"

I said, "My mother and grandma don't drive and my dad is working out of town. I need to get home and get back in school."

She said, "Why are you at a truck stop? You need to be at a bus station."

I said, "When I went to the bus station, they wouldn't let me take my bike. I was hoping a truck driver might be going to Dallas and let me ride with him and take my bike, too. I can pay for the ride. Do you know someone who might do that for me?"

She said she would check and see who was heading to Dallas and if they would take me. After a while, she came back and said she talked to a driver who was going to Dallas. He came over and asked me where I lived in Dallas. I guess I didn't answer fast enough because he said, "You don't know where you live?"

I didn't know what to say so I handed him the envelope with Eugene's address on it. He looked at me and said, "So you live in Oak Cliff?"

"Yeah."

"Okay, I can take you, but we won't get there until around midnight. You will have to spend the night at my house with my wife and two boys. My boys are eight and ten years old. Tomorrow I will take you in my car to your address in Oak Cliff."

He told the waitress that he would make sure I got there safely and not to worry about me. She gave me a piece of cake and didn't charge me. She said, "This one is for the road. Hold on to your money because you might need it where you're going."

I had no idea what she told the truck driver or what she thought about my story since my face was bruised and had a couple of bad cuts. She never asked me what happened to my face, but I think she and the truck driver knew I was running away from a dangerous situation.

We loaded up my bike and took off in a big semi-trailer truck. We didn't talk much because of the noise from the truck engine. It was late when we got to Dallas and his boys were asleep, but his wife was awake. She fixed a snack and then went to bed.

Hello Dallas

The next morning the trucker put my bike in the back of his pickup and took me to Eugene's house. He waited for me to see if anyone was home. I knocked on the door but became scared, thinking about how Eugene's mother might react when she saw me and if she would let me stay. I didn't know what to tell her about why I was here. Maybe I had made a big mistake coming here. My mind was racing when Mrs. Jones opened the door and saw me standing there. I froze and couldn't talk.

She says, "Floyd! Is that you?"

I was so overcome with so much emotion that I didn't say anything and started crying. She hugged me and I kept crying. I think it just hit me that I didn't have a family. I heard the truck driver walking up to ask Mrs. Jones if everything was okay. She asked him who he was and he introduced himself and said, "This is your son, right?"

She said, "No, but I know him."

"Where are his parents?" he asked. "He told me you were his mom. I thought I was just bringing him home."

She asked, "Has he been at your place very long?"

He said. "Oh no, I just picked him up in Altus, Oklahoma, yesterday. A waitress I've known a long time there asked me to give him a ride back to his family in Dallas."

Then Mrs. Jones turned toward me and asked me, "How did you know our address?" I handed her the letter from Eugene showing the address.

The truck driver gave her his name, address, and phone number and the waitress's name and the name of the truck stop. Then she told me to go inside, as she wanted to talk with the truck driver privately for a minute. I heard her ask him if he knew what happened to my face. He told her that was how I looked when he picked me up at the truck stop.

As the trucker drove away, Mrs. Jones came into the room and asked if I wanted to talk about what had happened to me. I didn't know what to say. If I told her the truth, would she believe me? I guess everything was just too much for me to handle because I started crying again. Mrs. Jones sat down beside me, gave me a hug and told me everything would be okay. After we sat there for a while, she took me into the kitchen and fixed me something to eat. Then we sat down at the table.

"I know what has happened to you because I've read some of the letters you sent to Eugene. After you finish eating you can go in the living room and lay on the sofa and watch TV. Eugene and his dad will be home around six. You can relax while I do some chores."

"Are you going to call my parents?"

"Well, you can talk! I thought something was wrong with your mouth. No, I'm not calling anyone. You can stay here for a while."

When Eugene and his dad came home that evening, they were surprised to see me. We had supper together and then Mrs. Jones told Eugene and me to go outside and find something to do while she talked with his dad. We went outside and to sit on his front porch. Eugene had a thousand questions for me.

"What are you doing in Dallas? How did you get here? Did J.D. do that to your face?"

"Yeah, he did it, but I don't want to talk about it right now. Can we just talk about something else?"

A little later, Mrs. Jones told us to come inside and go to bed. Nothing more was said about what happened to me.

The next morning, Eugene went to school but his dad didn't go to work. After Eugene left, Mr. & Mrs. Jones asked me to come in the living room so we could talk. I thought they were going to say I couldn't stay with them. I was thinking that I shouldn't have come here but should have gone to Oklahoma City where I had several friends and at least would have been close to Grandma and Uncle George if things didn't work out with my friends.

I sat down on the sofa and Mrs. Jones told me I could stay with them for the summer. At the end of summer, we would have the problem of my starting school in Dallas. The school would need information about my last school and my parents, which would probably tip off J.D. and Mom as to my whereabouts. Mrs. Jones told me she was afraid of getting in trouble for keeping me after school started.

I didn't know what to do. I didn't want to get Eugene and his family in trouble. I needed to think where to go after the summer was over and how to get there, but first I needed to find a place to hide the money I had stolen. I would need it when I left at the end of the summer.

The next day Mrs. Jones took me to the store and bought me enough clothes to get through the summer. The summer seemed to drag on, probably because I was always thinking about what I was going to do when it was over. Living with Eugene was a little boring because all we did was go to the movies and to the Lancaster-Kiest Shopping Mall. At first, the mall was new and exciting, but after a few visits, it was old news. Maybe it was just me. It was hard to have fun when I was always worrying and thinking about what was next after the summer was over. A few times, Eugene's parents took us out to eat. One place I really liked was a seafood restaurant on the north side of Dallas right by Harry Hines Boulevard on the traffic circle. The restaurant was built in the shape of an old ship.

When the summer was almost over, I needed to make some plans. I knew that Oklahoma City was the only place where I had friends who might take me in. A few days before school began, Mrs. Jones was going to take Eugene and me to the store to buy clothes for school. I pretended to be sick and told them I didn't feel like shopping. Mrs. Jones said she knew my sizes and what I needed so it was okay if I stayed home. She made a bowl of soup for me to eat if I got hungry. After they left, I rode my bike to a gas station to get a map. I returned to the house and spent the rest of the day planning my route to Oklahoma City. I learned that Highway 77 went to Oklahoma City and that it was also called Lancaster Road and was only a few blocks from Eugene's house. This road led to Oklahoma City, but I would have to hitchhike. This meant I couldn't take my bike.

It was almost time for Eugene and his mom to get home, so I hid the map under a drawer in the bathroom, and then put the drawer back in place. This was also where I kept my escape money. During these last few days of summer, I had to make my plans about when and how I could get away from the house, without the Jones' knowing about it. I would have to catch a time when Eugene and his mom went somewhere without me, and this was difficult because they always wanted me to go everywhere with them.

A few days later, Mrs. Jones told Eugene and me that she was going to downtown Dallas in the morning and that we could stay home and sleep late.

On the Move Again

After Eugene and I got up the next morning, he wanted us to go over to a friend's house and hang out. I told him to go ahead, because I was still tired and wanted to hang around the house. As soon as he left, I stuffed my clothes, map, and money in a paper sack and started walking toward Lancaster Road. As I was walking away, I looked back and saw my bike on the front porch. I hated to leave it, but there was no other way.

When I reached Lancaster Road, I put up my thumb to catch a ride. A few cars passed before one stopped and asked where I was going. I said I was going to meet my parents at the seafood restaurant over by the circle on Harry Hines. The woman asked me why I was hitchhiking instead of riding the bus. I told her my parents had given me money to ride the bus, but I had lost it. Her husband, who was driving, told me to get in, saying he was going close to the traffic circle. I climbed into the back seat with my big paper sack of clothes and was asked why I had a big bag of clothes. I had to think fast and told them I had been staying with my grandparents for a few days. Then I was asked why my grandparents weren't driving me to the circle. I told them they were too old to drive. The rest of the trip across town was very quiet. When we arrived at the restaurant, I was asked if I saw my parents' car. I said, "No, but I'm a little early so I'll just go inside and wait for them."

I was asked again if I would be okay and told them I would be fine. They drove off as I walked toward the door of the restaurant.

After they left, I walked to a gas station, bought a candy bar and a coke, and sat on a park bench in front of the gas station wondering what I would do if I couldn't get a ride or if no one was going to Oklahoma City. I was scared. This was different from riding my bike to Oklahoma City. So many things were going on in my mind. I decided to quit thinking about it or I would go crazy.

I got up, walked to the highway, set my bag down and put out my thumb. After a few cars went by, a car stopped and asked me where I was going.

"Oklahoma City."

Flying with Sailors
They said they were going only a couple of miles. I thanked them and waited for another ride.

In about thirty minutes, a car with four sailors stopped and asked me where I was going.

"Oklahoma City."

"Hop in. That's where we're going."

The back door opened. A sailor got out and told me to sit in the middle. He put my bag in the trunk then got back inside the car. He had barely shut the door when the driver took off like a bat out of hell, screeching the tires and fish-tailing down the road.

I noticed the smell of liquor. They were laughing and loud. The one on my right pulled out a bottle, took a big swig, then he handed the bottle to me.

"Have a drink, kid. Go ahead. It will put a smile on your face."

I took a sip. Today I know it was brandy and can almost taste it. As we passed the bottle around the car, everyone took a drink and soon the bottle was empty. One of the guys tossed the bottle out the window. By now I was pretty happy and we started to talk. I told them I was a runaway but they didn't believe me because of my size. I was twelve but small for my age. Most people would have guessed that I was ten.

Since I loved cars, I asked them what kind of car they were driving. They said it was a new 1950 Oldsmobile Eighty-Eight. I had never been in a car this nice.

Soon we were going super fast. I looked at the speedometer. We were doing 100 mph. At this speed, it didn't take us long to get to Oklahoma City. We arrived in the afternoon. I asked them to drop me off at my friend Rodney's house. When I arrived, Rodney was home and glad to see me. He asked me if I had moved back to Oklahoma City.

"Well, kinda."

"What do you mean?"

"I ran away from home and I hope your parents will let me stay for a few days."

"Boy, I don't know. Why did you run away?"

I told him the whole story. We must have talked for hours before his parents came home.

Rodney started telling them why I was there and asked if I could stay for a while. We talked for a long time as I told his parents my story. They said I could stay with them as long as I needed.

This was the first time in a long time I didn't need to think about what I was going to do next. I felt like everything was going to be okay, at least for a while.

I didn't know where his parents worked or what they did to make a living; I just knew they were gone almost every week for three or four days. His mother cooked a lot of food for us to eat while they were gone.

We were free to do almost anything we wanted—and when his parents were home, they didn't have a ton of rules. Rodney was my age but bigger, stocky, and a thug-looking guy. Everyone thought he was older than me and since I always looked younger, we didn't look like likely running mates. He was wild and crazy—one of those guys you could dare to do almost anything. We would go to dances, back then we called them "jam sessions". Rodney would randomly pick out a guard or policeman doing security, walk over to him, punch him in the face, and then run like crazy. He usually got away, too. He had no respect for anyone. His dad was a huge and crude big-mouth person, too, who would get in fist fights with Rodney.

Rodney had dark skin and hair, a deep voice and intimidated other students with his size and voice. We would roughhouse around sometimes like boys do, and since I was so much smaller, I would accidentally get hurt by him and really get mad at him. But he didn't care if he hurt me. When he fought anyone, he never showed angry emotions like me. Instead, he grinned like he really enjoyed hurting people.

Rodney didn't do well in school and eventually became a dropout. He was killed later after I went into the Air Force. Another friend, Barry, wrote and told me someone beat Rodney to death with a baseball bat. When I heard that, I felt so sad, as I knew if I hadn't married young and joined the Air Force that could have been me.

But back then, Rodney had a paper route, and I helped him with it while I lived with him. When his parents were out-of-town, we would stay out all night goofing off until it was time to pick up our papers at the paper station at 5 a.m.

Sometimes, we went to an area in Oklahoma City called "Packing Town" where two large meatpacking plants (Armor and Wilson) were located. Using slingshots we made from wood and straps we made from car tire inner tubes, we hunted pigeons behind the cattle lots. We would walk from one end of the lot to the other, scaring the pigeons into taking take flight. There were so many that we didn't need to aim-- just shoot, hitting one every time. We took them home and Rodney's mother cooked them for us.

Unsupervised Devilment

Each time his parents were out of town, we would think of more things to get into. One morning after we finished our paper route, we went to a restaurant in Packing Town called Cattleman's. We ordered a big breakfast. When we were almost finished, I told Rodney I needed to go to the bathroom. As I walked down the hall to the restroom, I noticed a back door. The idea struck me that we could go toward the restroom and walk out of the restaurant without paying. I told Rodney. He liked my idea, so I headed to the restroom after we finished eating and waited for Rodney. Then we both ran out the back door and down the alley as fast as we could.

We stopped running after a couple of blocks and talked about how much fun it was to skip paying the ticket. We started making a habit of this and went to the restaurant one or two times a week.

One day when we went in for breakfast and an older man took our order. When he brought our food, he sat down beside us and said in a calm voice, "Boys, this is your last free meal. Next time I will have some work for you to do before you get any food."

We continued to go to Cattleman's and eat, but we had to sweep the sidewalk, wash dishes, and other cleaning chores in the restaurant. When it was cold outside, it was good to sit in a warm restaurant and drink a cup of hot chocolate or have a hot meal. I had some tough years in my life, but I was learning that there were a lot of good people in the world.

Dream World vs Real World

After staying with Rodney and his family for several months, I thought I probably needed to move on. I don't know why I felt like this because Rodney's parents were good to me. I guess that schooling was the main reason. I was used to changing schools to keep from failing. It was the only way I knew to deal with my school problems and keep people from thinking I was dumb.

When Mother and I lived alone, I knew another family with two boys older than me on the northwest side of Oklahoma City. I used to spend the night and hang out with them. I decided to see if they would let me stay with them for a while. A few days after Christmas, I told Rodney that I was going to stay with the Martins for a while. Rodney didn't want me to go, and his parents said I could continue to stay with them as long as I wanted. I felt bad about leaving, but I had already told Leonard and Mrs. Martin that I was coming to stay with them. Also, I could change schools. I went to stay with the Martins in January and started a new school.

For the first few weeks, things were fine. Leonard was almost sixteen and had just gotten his first car. We cruised around in downtown Oklahoma City. For a thirteen-year-old, this was cool. Sometimes, however, I would find myself thinking about alone times Mom and I had together in Oklahoma City. I missed her and wondered if we would ever be close again. I worried about what she was going through with J.D. and if she understood why I left. I wrote her every month or two to tell her I was okay and not to worry about me. I didn't tell her why I left. I just couldn't. Many nights I lay in bed daydreaming about having a regular family with a mother, dad, brother, and sister. I dreamed about us going to the park or to the movies together.
I thought about how great it would be to get up the next morning to my dream family. Finally, I would tell myself that this dream world was not the real world and I would just have to make the best of it.

One day Leonard came home with a sled after a big snow. He said, "Let's go to the park and play in the snow." At the park, some big hills sloped down to a creek. We thought it would be great fun, with Leonard in front and me in the back. We took off down a big hill. The first part of the ride was great, but as we picked up speed, we hit pure ice and the sled began to spin until we were going down the hill backward and picking up speed.

As we reached the bottom, there was a steep grade on the other side. Since we were going down backward, the runners of the sled dug into the ice and we flew back, with Leonard landing on me, and my head slamming down on the ice. Leonard, checking to see if I was all right, saw blood on the ice by my head. He was big and husky and I was small, so he had no problem picking me up and carrying me two blocks to the house. He was scared, but Mrs. Martin decided it was not too bad.

During this time, I had a hard time in school. My grades were bad, and the teachers were always on my case for not knowing what I should know at my age. Some teachers put me down in class in front of the other students. I guess they thought this would shame me into trying harder, but all it did was cause the rest of the class to treat me badly and call me stupid. Because of this, I was a constant discipline problem—being a smart-off and starting fights. I didn't make many friends at this new school and started going back to Rodney's to visit on the weekends. Most of the time, his parents were out of town, so Rodney and I did anything we wanted to do. He was my best friend. He understood me. He still had his paper route, so I went with him to collect and throw the papers.

How a Poor Boy Makes Money

Saturday was collection day. A car-wrecking yard with hundreds of wrecked cars was in a field on his route. We hung out there drinking bottled cokes from an old coke machine for five cents. One day a man came in and asked the owner if he had a radio for his Buick. The old man who operated the place said he didn't have one. I remembered seeing an old wrecked Buick beside a house on Rodney's paper route. The grass was growing underneath it, so it had been parked there for quite a while. As the man walked out the door, I told the old guy behind the counter that I knew where a radio was in a wrecked Buick and thought I could get it for him. He ran out to catch the man in the driveway and told him he could have a radio for him in a few days. He told me he would pay me ten dollars for the radio if I had it by Monday.

I had to think fast because I didn't want him to know that we had to wait until dark to steal it. I said, "I don't think the owner will be there today, but I can bring it by tomorrow."

He said, "No, tomorrow is Sunday and we aren't open. But I live next door, so just bring it and bang on my door."

So this was a new way for me to make some money and I took advantage of it.

But then I got an even better idea on how to get a car radio. One day we were walking down a street and I pointed out a Buick several blocks away in a driveway.

I said, "Just think, we can make ten bucks in about thirty minutes. It takes over a week to make that much on your paper route!"

Rodney said, "I thought you were talking about a wrecked car in a backyard—not a new car in a driveway."

"Never mind what I said. We'll come back after dark. I have taken out radios before, so I know what tools we'll need to take out the radio. Here's the plan: we'll be casual when we walk down the street. When we reach the car, we look around and make sure no one is watching. If the coast is clear, we duck down between the car and hedge. When I open the car door, you have to push the button that turns off the dome light. You have to be very quick, because the longer the dome light stays on, the greater the chance that we'll get caught. You'll have to hold the dome light button while I take out the radio. We also need to bring a newspaper bag to put the radio in, so we can walk down the street like nothing has happened. You got that?"

"Yeah! I got it!"

"Okay, make sure you don't talk or make any noise. Remember to hold the dome button down."

Everything went as planned and we got the radio and took it to the wrecking yard to collect our ten bucks. This was easy money. Maybe I could do this more often. So Rodney and I began hanging out at the wrecking yard, hoping someone would come in needing a car part that the old man didn't have in the yard.

Days later, we hadn't had any luck, so I asked the old man if there was anything we could find for him. He told us that a man came in looking for a set of hubcaps for a Cadillac.

He said he would give us seven dollars for each one, but he needed all four and they had to match.

Looking back now, I can see the old man was setting us up to steal car parts for him. I didn't catch on at the time and thought I was really cool for coming up with this grand moneymaking scheme! A few days later, I saw some Cadillac hubcaps on the north side of Oklahoma City. This job would be a little harder than most because the four hubcaps were large and difficult to haul across town without drawing attention.

I knew I could put two in one large canvas bag we used to haul newspapers from the paper station. The bag had a long strap that slipped over the shoulder. This was handy when throwing papers from a bike. We could carry all four hubcaps if we each carried a bag. At times like this, I really missed my bike. It would be easier to ride across town with the hubcaps on a bike instead of trying to hitchhike with them.

That evening, I threw a large screwdriver into a bag to pop the hubcap off and a couple of other tools. We walked down Western Street, one of the main streets in Oklahoma City. We quickly caught a ride and got dropped off about two blocks from the Cadillac with the hubcaps.
It was 9:30 p.m. and a dark night. We didn't see anyone as we walked down the street. The car was parked on the street, not in the driveway. I took out my screwdriver to pop the hubcap off and told Rodney to stand close by with the bag as I popped it off. It made a loud popping noise. I looked around but didn't see anyone as I put it in the bag. Also, no lights came on in the nearby houses. I worked as fast as I could, popping off the other three hubcaps, making a loud noise each time.

With our bags, we ran around the corner, down the alley, and hid in a dark place. We had been there for about fifteen minutes when Rodney started pushing to leave.

"No," I said. "We need to stay here longer just in case anyone heard the noise and called the police."

From our hiding place, were able to see if a police car drove down the street and would have time to duck behind an old storage building.

We stayed another fifteen minutes then went down the alley for several blocks before heading over to Western Street to catch a ride back to the south side of town.

A man picked us up and asked what we had in our bags. Since it was too late to be throwing newspapers, I had to think up something fast. I told him that we went to my grandmother's house after we threw our papers and were bringing back some things she was sending to my mother. The rest of the evening we had fun goofing off after we stashed the hubcaps in the bushes by Rodney's house. The next day we took the hubcaps to the wrecking yard and got our twenty-eight dollars, a small fortune to me at the time.

Today I own a 1963 Thunderbird. When I pop off a hubcap to work on it, the popping noise transports me back to that moment—standing there, scared to death, with my heart racing fast, hoping no one heard the sound.

That summer, Rodney and I hung out with each other, walking around town looking for things to steal and sell to the wrecking yard. As time went on, we got bolder and Rodney did things that I thought might get us caught. For example, if we passed a car parked on the side of the street, Rodney would smash out the windows with a crowbar (we carried a crowbar to pry things open and to take wheels and tires off cars) and make a lot of noise. Lights would come on in houses all around us and we would have to run as fast as we could for three or four blocks. I would be mad at Rodney and start telling him how stupid he was, but he would just laugh and say, "What's wrong? Can't you handle a little excitement?" In a way, I must have liked it too, because I didn't stop running with him. We carried on our petty thief routine for the rest of the summer.

Blowing Money on Whiskey

One Saturday evening shortly before school started, Rodney came up with an idea to buy some bootlegged liquor. He said he knew about an old house in Packing Town. You go to the back, knock on a window, and when it opened, you slide five dollars onto the windowsill and someone slides back a bottle of whiskey.

I asked him how he knew about this place. He told me that he overheard some older boys talking about it. Five dollars was a lot of money in the early 50s, but we had more than thirty dollars from our stealing venture and money from Rodney's paper route. I was only thirteen years old, but all this money made me think I was on top of the world.

When we got to Packing Town, we found the old house. It was surrounded by overgrown trees and a bunch of junk cars in the backyard. It was dark and spooky and I wanted to leave, but Rodney wanted the whiskey. We went to the house and knocked on the window but couldn't see inside because the window was higher than our heads. The window opened and a voice said, "What do you boys want?"

Rodney said, "Whiskey."

"You got five dollars?"

Rodney slid it across the windowsill and the window closed.

I wondered if we were being swindled and not going to get anything. In a few minutes, the window opened with a hand coming out holding a bottle of whiskey. We took the half-pint back to Rodney's house, taking sips on the way. The whiskey burned my throat at first and almost took my breath away. However, by the time we got to Rodney's house, I was feeling no pain and my throat wasn't burning either. We were feeling a buzz and just kept on drinking.

Suddenly, I felt sick. At the same time, Rodney's parents came home. They guessed why I was sick and told me they needed to take me home—which meant the Martins' house on the north side of town. The Martins were church-going people and would be very unhappy with me showing up drunk. I asked Rodney's mom if I could stay all night and she said no because she was mad at both of us for drinking. I told her I didn't think I could ride in a car without throwing up. They put me in the car anyway and away we went to the Martins' house. Rodney stayed home because he was sick, too.

When we arrived at the Martins' house, Rodney's mom knocked on the door. I don't know what she told Mrs. Martin, but when they came to get me out of the car, Mrs. Martin was not happy with me. They had to help me out of the car because I was so sick and dizzy. I knew I had really messed up because the Martins had been very good to me and I had let them down.

I don't know if it was just feeling guilty about what I did or if the Martins felt differently toward me after my self-induced sickness. Because from that time on, things were not the same with them, so after school was out, I went to live with Grandma and Uncle George. They had moved to a small house on the corner of 23rd and Blackwelder Street in the west part of Capitol Hill in Oklahoma City. This actually put me closer to Rodney, and we hung out together more than ever that summer.

Homeless Leads to New Girl "Friend"
Toward the end of the summer, I heard that Mom and J.D. were coming to town. I couldn't be at Grandma's house when they arrived, so I stayed at Rodney's for a couple of days while his parents were out of town, then I went to the paper station and stayed a couple of nights. I decided not to stay with anyone for more than two or three days. I developed some friends down at the paper station who knew I was sleeping there and sometimes they would ask me to spend a night or two with them too. I still managed to stay at Rodney's two or three nights a week.

One day when we slept late, Rodney's mom came home and realized I was staying there while they were out of town. I expected her to be mad, but she wasn't and said that was why she had been leaving extra food when they were out of town. She said I was welcome to stay, but I still didn't want to wear out my welcome, so I only stayed a few days at a time.

I sometimes stayed with another friend in town, Raymond, who lived in a duplex. A pretty girl named Julie lived on the other side of the duplex. A long porch crossed the front with doors to both sides of the duplex. Julie, who was taller and older than me, would come out and sit on her side of the porch. She had blue eyes, a pretty face, and a cute figure. She also wore tight clothes, tight shorts, and tops in the summer and liked to flaunt her cute body. I would watch for her to come out on the porch so I could go over and talk with her.

She told me her mother died when she was ten and she lived with her dad, who worked for a tractor company as a mechanic. I told her that I ran away from home because my step-dad beat me. I was about to be fourteen and she sixteen and we both had birthdays in March. We became good friends and sat on the porch a lot after school. She began inviting me into her house and making sandwiches for me.

One day Raymond told me that his parents did not like me talking to Julie or going over to her house. They wouldn't let him come out when she was visiting with me on the porch. I asked Raymond if he was mad at me for not spending as much time with him. He said, "Well, you kind of spend most of your time with her whenever you come over to my house." I asked him why he didn't like her. He said he didn't really know, but his mom and dad didn't like her. I told Julie that I wouldn't be able to visit as much because Raymond's parents were mad at me.

Julie was lonely because her Dad was gone a lot. She said I could sneak in the back door to visit her and no one would know I was there. I continued to see her several times a week. On the nights I went to see her, I slept in the paper station because none of the families I stayed with liked me coming in late at night.

Rodney was mad at me because I wasn't spending as much time with him. We still went out a couple nights a week to steal something, as it was my only way to have some spending money.

Not much changed for me during the next few months. By spending a few nights with different friends, their parents were unaware that I didn't have a real home. However, going from one home to another was beginning to get old. It was not as much fun as it was at first. Julie's house was the only place where I didn't feel like I was imposing.

Julie's dad had bought her a car. As the weather got colder, she would pick me up at Rodney's so I didn't have to walk in the cold. Christmas was fast approaching and I had no idea about what I would do for Christmas. Julie said I could spend Christmas with her and her dad. I had met him a couple of times and he seemed very nice, but I really wanted to be with someone from my family. I decided to go to Grandma's and Uncle George's for Christmas and stay a few days. I hoped that Mom and J.D. wouldn't show up. We always had aunts, uncles, and cousins at Grandma's house for Christmas and I really wanted to see them all. I really wanted to see Mom too, but knew I couldn't because of J.D.—and I lucked out because they didn't come that Christmas.

Two Christmas Celebrations

Everyone was surprised to see me. I enjoyed visiting with my family, especially on Christmas Day. A lot of the family members scarcely knew me. They hadn't seen me for several years. I told them that I had been living with a great family in Oklahoma City and they had really been good to me. That afternoon, I called Julie to pick me up and I left a little early on Christmas Day. I wanted my family members to think I was living the good life, so I told them I had to get back and have Christmas dinner with my new family.

We went to Julie's. Her dad was home, and our *fabulous* Christmas dinner was some sandwiches made by Julie. Her dad told me that I was welcome to stay with them as long as I needed. He said Julie had told him about how I had run away from home and was living with friends. I told him that I would stay with them some but not all the time because I shared a paper route with a friend which took me away three days a week. He insisted that I stay with them whenever possible and told Julie to make up a bed for me in the back bedroom. They didn't know that my part of a paper route was really stealing things with Rodney.

I started staying at Julie's house most of the time and staying at Rodney's only when his parents were out of town.

Upping the Ante—Wrecking Yard—Wrecking My Nerves

Rodney and I had advanced into stealing bigger and better things. After almost getting caught stealing from cars parked on the street, I started thinking of a better way. Rodney and I walked by an auto repair shop that did high-performance upgrades. We stopped, admired, and looked under the hood if it was open. A thought hit me when we saw new engine parts. I bet we could sell some of these new parts for more money, but we needed to figure out a way to get inside the shop.

We went to the wrecking yard and I told the man that I had a friend who had a high-performance intake manifold with three carburetors and that he needed money and had to sell it. I asked the man if he would like to buy it. He asked me how much my friend wanted. I countered by asking what he would give for it. He said he would give seventy-five dollars for one in excellent shape. I told him that I would bring it by if my friend would sell it for that amount.

Acting like we were looking at the cars, Rodney and I went to the auto shop that afternoon to check out the place. I noticed that the back door had a big padlock. There was no way we could get in that way, but I thought I could get in the front door with a screwdriver. We waited until midnight when there was little traffic on the road in front of the shop. I would need to be quick opening the door before anyone drove by and saw us. This was a new challenge, as we had never broken into a building. I decided to do it on a Sunday night when fewer people would be out and about. I went over the plan several times with Rodney to make sure that we both knew our specific jobs.

When we decided that it was time to do it, we went down the alley to the back of the shop, down the side of the building, and around to the front door. Rodney stood by the corner of the building and watched for cars coming down the street. While I jimmied the door open, Rodney saw a car, and I had to scramble fast to hide behind a car sitting in the driveway. Luckily, no more cars showed up. We continued trying to break into the building. We only had a couple of canvas newspaper bags and a screwdriver, but I knew there would be tools inside the shop that we could use to remove the manifold from a car. We were in luck. They had a manifold ready for installation. The linkage, however, was not hooked up and only a few bolts were holding the manifold in place. In a few minutes, I had it ready to come off, but I didn't count on its weight. It would not fit in our canvas bags.

I asked Rodney if he could carry it a little way down the alley. He picked it up while I opened the door. We went around the building and down the alley to where I saw some bushes. I told Rodney to put it down while we thought of a way to get it to the wrecking yard. We sat there for a few minutes.

Rodney said, "I know where Dad keeps an extra set of keys to the car. They're hanging in the garage."

I said, "Let's do it!"

We used the brush from the nearby bushes to cover the manifold and went to Rodney's house for the keys. Rodney knew how to drive because his dad lets him drive down the back streets with him. The only problem was that his dad was home. I was afraid he would wake up when Rodney started the car. So we put the car in neutral and pushed the car down the driveway and down the street a ways before we started the car.

When we get back to the place we hid the manifold, we didn't want to attract attention, so we didn't drive down the alley. Instead, we parked by the alley in the street and walked down the alley and carried the manifold to the car. We loaded the manifold as fast as we could and returned to Rodney's house. When we got close to Rodney's house we turned off the lights and the car motor and coasted into the driveway. We unloaded it and put it beside the garage under some bushes. Rodney said, "What are we going to do with it now?"

"I'll think of something by morning. Meanwhile, go in before your dad sees that you are not in bed. I'll see you at the paper station in the morning."

The next morning when I met Rodney at the paper station, he told me that his parents were leaving town at noon. Now we didn't have a car to transport the manifold to the wrecking yard.

We worked the paper route then went to Cattleman's Restaurant for breakfast. I now had plenty of money and could pay for my breakfast. As we tried to figure out how to get the manifold to the wrecking yard, Rodney said he knew a guy with a car who might help us. I said, "No, I don't want anyone besides us to know anything about this deal. It ain't safe because people always tell their friends and pretty soon everyone knows about it and we get caught!"
Then it occurred to me that he may have already told someone about our stealing and selling at the wrecking yard. I asked and he said, "No."

I said, "I don't believe you!" I was so mad that I walked out of the restaurant.

Rodney followed me out and said, "Don't be mad. I promise I didn't tell anyone."

I said, "You better not tell. If you tell one person, we can end up in jail! I don't want to go to jail."

We hung around until we thought Rodney's parents were gone then went to his house. Rodney checked to see if they had taken all their travel stuff and let me know that the coast was clear. We put the manifold in the garage and cleaned it.

We went to the wrecking yard and told the man that the guy brought it to our house but it was too heavy for us to carry. We asked him if he could pick it up at our house. He agreed to come by after work. So we went back to the wrecking yard at 6 p.m. and rode with him to Rodney's house. He got the manifold and we got the seventy-five dollars. This was the most money we had ever made on a deal, but it had been hard to pull off. I knew I had to come up with a better plan next time.

Young Love—First Love

I liked staying at Julie's house. Not only was her dad good to me, but she took me riding around town in her car. I always bought the gas, and we would stop at a drive-in for burgers and cokes.

When I was growing up, there were a bunch of drive-in burger joints like today's Sonic Drive-Ins but they had large parking lots, some holding as many as one hundred cars. They were great meeting places for young people. We hung out with them for an hour or two nearly every evening during the summer months. Sometimes we got out of our cars and sat on the hoods. I thought it was great to hang out with older students. Each night I stayed with Julie, we hung out at a drive-in. She liked it because I had plenty of money to pay for everything. Her dad was good to her but didn't have enough money to give her many extras. He gave her a dollar a week for gas to go back and forth to school. Gas was only sixteen cents a gallon, so she got about a hundred miles out of that dollar.

One night after we came home around 10 p.m. Julie told me that her dad had made a new batch of home brew (he always made his own beer). She said this was one of the best batches he had ever made and she asked me if I wanted to try some.

"Sure, but what if your dad comes home and finds us drinking his beer?"

"He ain't coming home tonight because he has so much paperwork. He's spending the night at his office. He always tells me this, but I know he is just spending the night with his girlfriend. Besides, he doesn't care if we drink a little of his beer."

She told me that her dad would pour her a beer and they would sit and drink together and that was when they had their best talks.

She got the beer and we sat close to each other on the sofa talking. I told her she was lucky to have a dad that loved her and I would give anything to have a dad like hers. She grabbed me and gave me a big hug. Then she gave me a big kiss. I had kissed girls before, but this kiss was very different.

After that night, we became very close and I didn't want to go to Rodney's house anymore. But I had to keep running around with him so I would have some money. During this time, my life was so different than when I lived with J.D. that it almost felt like a dream. I think it was because I was so happy and had fallen in love with Julie. Julie and I had birthdays in March. I was turning fourteen and she would be sixteen. One day her dad asked me if I could be at their house on Sunday afternoon. He wanted to take Julie and me to a birthday dinner at a fancy cafeteria with really good food. I didn't stay Saturday night because I needed to get some parts for the wrecking yard for Monday.

I arrived a little before noon on Sunday to find Julie standing on the front porch in a new blue dress that matched her eyes perfectly. I was stunned and just stood there for a moment admiring this blonde beauty. Her dad asked me why I was just standing in the front yard and motioned me to come in the house. He told me to come into the bedroom where he had a birthday gift for me. It was a nice blue dress shirt that was almost the color as Julie's blue dress. I put on the shirt. It was the nicest shirt I had ever owned.

We went to the cafeteria and got in line. I had never seen this much food in one place and wished I could have eaten some of everything. Her dad decided to help me. With his help, I got more food than I could eat. This was an exciting experience. Even today when I go to a cafeteria, I remember that day.

I continued to stay at Julie's house whenever I could until one day her dad came in and told us he had been transferred to Kansas City and they would be moving at the end of the school year in two weeks. The two weeks passed fast before I had time to adjust to the idea of Julie moving away. I knew I had to adjust, as I had adjusted to other life's disappointments in my life. As they were loading their belongings, Julie told me she would write me. I waved goodbye as they drove off. I never received a letter or heard from her again. I still wonder what happened to her and how her life turned out. She was a friend I really needed at that time in my life.

Licenses Make Old Habits Easier

I began spending most of my time with Rodney and his parents after school was out. His parents let me stay three or four days a week again. Rodney and I roamed the streets looking for something to steal. One day, his dad came in and told Rodney he was going to get him a car so we could expand our paper route business. I didn't know that Rodney had been telling his dad that if he had a car we could probably double our paper subscriptions. His dad said we would have to get our driver's licenses in Texas where they issue them at age fourteen. In Oklahoma, we needed to be fifteen and a half years old. We loved the idea of having a car and could scarcely wait until the next Monday when we'd go to Texas.

We drove to Wichita Falls, Texas. Driver's license requirements were very lenient in the early 1950s. Rodney's dad had only to show his driver's license for Rodney to get a license. Since I had a different last name, his Dad had to explain that I lived with them and vouch for my correct name. We took our driver's test and got our licenses. The next day, Rodney's dad bought him a 1942 Chevy for seventy-five dollars. The car was almost worn out, but we knew how to fix it up and steal parts for it, too. By now we were stealing tires, wheels, carburetors and generators. Once, we took a radiator out of a car in a used car lot. The car was located in the back corner of the lot in a dark spot by the alley. We spent about an hour removing it and lifting it over the back fence into the alley. We drove Rodney's car up the alley and loaded it up for delivery to the wrecking yard the next day.

The summer went by very fast as we stayed busy with our stealing, making about one hundred dollars every week and a few times we made over two hundred. This was really good money to make in the 1950's when the average paycheck for a grown man was about fifty dollars a week. During the summer, I got tired of depending on Rodney for my transportation and decided to save enough money to buy my own car. As we were going down 29th street one day, I saw a black 1949 Ford Coupe with whitewall tires and some moon hubcaps. I told Rodney to pull into the car lot so I could look at the car. I knew immediately this was the car I wanted.

I asked the salesman if I could test-drive it. He didn't want to let me at first, but I convinced him that I could come up with the money if I liked the way it drove. We left Rodney's car at the lot and took off in the Ford. As we drove out of the drive, Rodney asked me where I was going to get the money to buy a car. He didn't know that all this time, he was only getting a small part of the money from our auto part sales. But he was getting most of the money from his paper route. I told him I would be able to borrow the money from my Uncle George.

I had over six hundred dollars hidden in a coffee can in Rodney's dad's garage. We only drove around a few minutes and I went back to the car lot where the salesman and I began haggling over the price. He wanted four hundred fifty and we settled on four hundred. We went back to Rodney's house and as we pulled into the drive, I knew I had to think of a way to get Rodney out of the garage so I could get my money. I told him I thought his car was getting hot and he needed to go into the house and get a bucket filled with water while I checked the radiator. It worked and I was able to get my money from the coffee can.

I asked him to take me to my Uncle George's house. When we got there, I went in for a few minutes and left Rodney in the car. When I came out, I waved the money at him that he thought I borrowed the money from my Uncle George, and said, "So let's go get my car."

Back then buying a car was like shopping at any store. I handed the man the cash and he gave me the keys and the title and we were done. As soon as Rodney's dad got back in town, he helped me with putting the car in my name and getting insurance. School was about to start and it was going to be great to have my own car. Not many kids my age had their own car. Having my car helped me forget how hard it was not to have Julie around anymore because I had become very close to her.

Joy Rides and Close Calls

My '49 Ford was really nice. It was a Club Coupe that was sportier than the four-door and had a good radio (a lot of cars back then didn't have radios). It had whitewall tires and the motor was very fast. I could usually outrun most of the other kids' cars in drag races.

On the first day of school, Rodney and I showed up in my Ford, which I was really looking forward to showing off. Since we were new at this school, we didn't have any friends yet. There was a place across the street from the school where all the tough kids hung out called "Speeds." Rodney and I decided to check it out. There were about twenty to twenty-five high school students hanging around and most were older than us and were seniors in high school. We just stood around looking at everyone. Most of them seemed to have other friends and we felt like outsiders. We had only been there a few minutes when I heard some yelling and looked up to see Rodney punch an eleventh-grade boy in the face.

The fight was on and this guy had a lot of friends. I was standing there, wondering if or when some of his friends were going to jump into the fight, because if they did, I would have to step into it, too. But we were lucky because none of them did. I was glad because there were so many of them that we would have gotten the crap beaten out of us. Rodney didn't have much trouble beating this guy and we just strolled off, not even looking back, as though we were not afraid of the other guys. After that, we got a rough reputation and attracted students from the group and started hanging out with some of them.

I had an auto mechanics class and some of this group was in my class. Rodney didn't like auto mechanics, so he didn't join me in the three-hour afternoon class. When school was out, I would hang out with my new friends and sometimes Rodney would hang out with us too. He didn't like most of my new auto mechanic friends and would not always come with us. I think he really liked it when he was my only friend. We still hung out on the weekends and kept up our stealing.

We started stealing cars to take joy rides. We always stole the fancy cars like Cadillacs, Lincolns, and Oldsmobiles. These luxury cars were big enough for eight to ten teens if we squeezed in real tight. We could get five people in the front and five in the back. We did this once or twice a month. Actually, we had this stealing routine down to a science. We would go to a car lot and I would get the salesperson to take me out on the lot to look at a car. Rodney would look for the keys to a car we wanted to drive later that night. Back then, all the car keys in a sales lot were kept on a pegboard on a wall in the office and each key had a tag identifying the car. Rodney would pick a key from the board.

We would go back around 10 p.m. and just drive the car off the lot. Rodney would follow me to the place we were going to park my car and leave the other car when we were through with our joy drive. This worked really good until one night we were cruising around after we had dropped off our buddies and I saw red flashing lights coming up behind me. Now, my heart started beating really fast. I drove a couple of blocks before I pulled over. I didn't know what I would say to the cop and, as I was trying to think up something, the cop came to my window and said, "Where did you get this car?"

I sat there for a minute and then stepped on the gas and took off. I made a hard right turn at the next block. My car was parked only a few blocks away and I knew I had to ditch this car quick and get to my car. I made a hard left at the next block and as I turned, I looked back and didn't see any red light. I turned off all the car lights and began driving in the dark. I saw a driveway going up between two houses. As I turned to hit the driveway, I hit the curb and I bounced almost off the seat. But I made it to the driveway, running the car between the two houses.

Rodney and I bailed out as fast as we could and hit the alley running. We had to cross a couple of streets before we got to my car and slowed down just enough to see if any cop cars were around. As we crossed the streets to reach where my car was parked, we hid behind some shrubs to make sure there were no cop cars coming…then we ran and jumped in my car. Before I got it started, I saw a cop car coming down the street. We ducked down in the seat as low as we could and saw the cop car go flying by us. We sat there a moment and I started the motor while I was still ducked down in the seat. I raised my head up very slowly and told Rodney to lie down. I didn't see anything, so I turned my headlights on and started to pull away from the curb slowly and drive calmly for the next few blocks so I wouldn't attract any attention.

Once we were in the clear, I told Rodney he could sit up now. That was enough excitement for one night and I was ready to go home. That night we stayed awake talking about how close we came to getting caught. The next day, Rodney's dad started telling us about an article in the newspaper about how the cops had almost caught the teenagers that had been stealing cars from area car lots. We decided to lay off stealing joy rides for a while. The whole ordeal scared me so much that

I didn't want to do any more stealing because the thought of going to jail for a long time was very frightening to me.

Things Have Got to Change

I still had a few hundred dollars in my stash, so I decided to use it and just do the paper route with Rodney for a little extra money. If I didn't have any car repairs, I would be okay. The rest of the year was pretty boring, getting up at 5 a.m. and throwing papers and then going to school. After school, we did our paper collections and just hung out at the drugstore. Rodney was getting tired of just hanging out at the drugstore and started running with some other boys. He wanted me to come along, but I said no. We still did the morning paper route together but I had become good friends with Frankie who was in my shop class.

Frankie was a small guy, even shorter than me. The girls really liked him and thought he was quite a looker. He was blond with a small build, soft-spoken but he liked to fight. He was a good mechanic like me but wasn't crazy like Rodney. When we did our petty crimes or joy rides, he was careful like me because he didn't want to get caught. He didn't have a dad, just lived with his mom, who was a partying lady who stayed out all night with different boyfriends.

After I served in the Air Force for six years and returned to the Oklahoma City area, I found he had changed and gotten into drugs. I was married then with two daughters, so we had to go our separate ways. After a few years, I moved with my family to Dallas and it was while I was there I got word Frankie had died. It was ruled an accident, but we all thought different. The story told was that he was going around a corner too fast and fell out of his car. My buddies and I thought maybe some rival had knocked him in the head, drove his car and threw him out of it. Even to this day, I mourn for the fourteen-year-old who was such a good friend to me.

Back then our gang would cut class about one or two times a week and go to Turner Falls or a nearby park just to hang out and have fun. Sometimes we would drive over to another school in Oklahoma City to stir up a fight with a rival gang for extra excitement. We called our gang the Bo Diddlies after a popular singer "Bo Diddley" in the early 50's.

One of our gang was beaten to death with a baseball bat, one went to prison for stabbing and killing a person in a bar and after he got out, was shot and killed by his girlfriend.

Another gang member died in his late 20s. He was found sitting in his parked car with a gunshot wound to his head. It was ruled a suicide but he was shot behind his left ear and he was right handed. One member just disappeared and was never heard from again. Only one gang member besides me lived past the age of 30.

Christmas Gift: A Teacher Cares

But now back to my teenage self. Christmas was almost here again. I had no plans because Rodney and I didn't hang much anymore. I spent most of my nights at the paper station which had a good heater and some benches for me to sleep on. I had a car and a little money, but not having a home to go to was getting very lonely. I asked Frankie if I could stay with him for maybe a month or so but his mom said no. I always went by to see my Grandma and Uncle George a couple times a month but didn't stay long because I never knew if J.D. and Mom might show up.

The closer Christmas got, the more I began to worry about what I was going to do. I couldn't take a chance of running into J.D. at my grandmother's house. I thought, *was I going to be all by myself on Christmas Day?* Sometimes I would just have to make myself stop thinking about how much J.D. had ruined my life! Other times I would daydream about someday seeing him sitting in his car. I would just walk up and shoot him in the back of the head or I would daydream about what I would do if he was visiting at my grandmother's house.

I imagined that I would get some of my buddies and park close by, but out of sight. We would wait for J.D. to go to the store by himself, which he probably would do because he always bought bootleg liquor and secretly drank when Mom wasn't around. We would follow him to the store and I would sneak into the back seat and wait for him to come out of the store. I would hold a gun to his head and make him drive to a secluded place out in the country. My buddies would follow me in their car and we would beat him and torture him for a long time and then I would kill him. I hated him so much I wasn't sure I might really carry out this plan if I saw him again. He had completely ruined my life and stopped me from being able to see my mom.

But I could not take a chance of letting my anger get the best of me. Besides, I didn't want to be locked up in jail for the rest of my life for murder, either. For the next few days, I kept myself really busy to keep from thinking about how much I hated J.D. I would have nightmares about these daydreams, too.

I guess my guardian angel knew how much I wanted to have a Family Christmas Dinner because just a few days before Christmas, Mr. Jameson, the shop teacher, called me aside and said he heard me talking to some of the other students about not having any place to go for Christmas Dinner and he asked me if I would like to come to his house. He told me it would be just him, his wife and two boys. I asked how old are your two boys and he said ages five and six. I was so stunned that I just sat there for a minute and finally Mr. Jameson said, "I guess that means a yes?"

And I said, "Yes, sir!"

For the next few days, I felt better about my life, since Mr. Jameson had asked me over to his house on Christmas Day. He told me to come by around 11 a.m. When I arrived, they had finished opening all their gifts and the boys were showing me what they got. Soon dinner was ready, and it was one of the best meals I had eaten in a long time. After dinner, Mr. Jameson asked his boys to go to their rooms because he and Mrs. Jameson wanted to talk to me. We went in the living room and sat down on the sofa and Mrs. Jameson asked me where I was living. I didn't know what to say for a minute or two. Finally, I said I was staying with friends.

I think Mr. Jameson knew I was just staying anywhere possible because he probably overheard me talking to some kids in class about it. So Mrs. Jameson asked me if I would like to stay with them. She said I could have my own bedroom and then she came over and gave me a hug and said she thought I would be happy here. She said, "Why don't you go get your things from your friend's house so you can start staying with us today?"

I said, "All I own is with me in my car."

So Christmas, 1952, I moved in with the Jameson's family. I only had a few changes of clothes and the dirty ones were in the trunk of my car with the clean ones just lying in the back seat. We brought them in and Mrs. Jameson came in my bedroom and picked up most of my clothes and said, "I will just put these in the washing machine for you and they will be ready for you in the morning."

The next couple of days I just stayed in the house playing with their boys and the new toys they got for Christmas. Mr. Jameson didn't want me getting up so early and staying out late working on my paper route because he felt it interfered with my school attendance. I quit my paper route and got a job at a nearby Safeway Grocery Store bagging groceries.

Back then, we had to bag the groceries and carry the bags to the car for the customer. The manager was always giving me a hard time because I didn't move fast enough for him and run when I worked. After the store closed, we had to clean up and that took an hour or hour and a half and then we would have a meeting, but our time was always cut off as soon as the store closed. At one of these meetings, he said I was too slow and should walk a lot faster when I worked. All the other baggers knew he was not fair by making us stay late and not paying us, but didn't have the guts to say anything. We had to line up in a row and he called me over to him and I just walked slowly and then he called another bagger and he ran to him.

He said, "You see? That is how I want you to walk." I told him to kiss my ass and walked out because I knew I would be fired.

But while working at the grocery store, I met Mr. Hinner, the pharmacist at the drugstore next door, who had always been friendly to me. I went to his store and shared my story of quitting the grocery store and he hired me to deliver prescription drugs to people's home with my car. I made deliveries for him every day after school. Some days I didn't even have any deliveries to make and just set in the back of the store working on model cars, but I still got paid.

The Jamesons were very good to me, so I started staying at home with them a lot and just enjoying family life with them. I continued living with them until the summer of 1953. The beginning of that summer I went to visit Grandma & Uncle George and they told me that Mom and J.D. had moved to Arizona. I knew they would not be coming back to visit that summer, so I moved back in with Grandma and Uncle George. They lived near Capitol Hill now and were only about five blocks from my job at the drugstore and about eighteen blocks from my high school. I continued living with them when school started the next year and I was in the eleventh grade. I was still in Mr. Jameson's auto mechanics class and he would invite me to dinner every once in a while.

I always had a good relationship with Mr. Jameson and his family, even after I was married and moved away from Oklahoma City. Whenever I came back to town, I would go visit him.

Back to Old Stealing Tricks

I still worked for Mr. Hinner for twelve dollars a week. That was for working every evening after school and on Saturday, which added up to about twenty or twenty-two hours a week. That was okay for a kid my age but I missed having a lot of money, so it was not long before I started my old habits again. I started hanging out with Frankie and going by the auto wrecking yard. We quickly found out some things the owner needed.

We were back to our old tricks, stealing anything we could sell to the wrecking yard owner. I was back in the money again. I still worked for the pharmacy until 6 or 6:30 every evening. Most of the time, I would tell Uncle George and Grandma I was spending the night at Frankie's house. That way I could run around stealing all night, skip school the next day, and take Frankie home in the morning. Then I would just find myself a place to park and sleep in my car. We did this a couple times a week. School was just not important to me.

I often wonder how well I would have done in school if I had gotten a good start. In my younger years, I went to public school and made good grades. But later on, Mom put me in the non-certified Pentecostal church school where I quickly began to fall behind because the school was just a joke. After she married J.D. we moved all the time, so I was behind in all subjects except for math, which came easy for me. The teachers at Capitol Hill High School passed me, I think because I was always starting trouble in their class by fighting or telling the teacher off and walking out of class. By passing me, they were making sure I would not be in their class again!

Looking back, I see how I let my anger for J.D keep me from even trying to do good in school. My anger kept me from seeing how a good education would help me later in life. If I had taken my schoolwork seriously, my life would have been easier later on. I had the math aptitude to go to college but I didn't read and write good enough. Years later I learned that I was slightly dyslexic and couldn't read beyond an eight- grade level. But my lack of education never stopped my entrepreneurial spirit or kept me out of the business world.

The school year didn't change much. I hung out with Frankie doing our regular work of stealing car parts and selling them to make ourselves extra money. Then one day, Frankie and I decided to try a new type of stealing. We were going to break into houses to steal stuff we could fit in our pockets, like jewelry, watches, and money. First, we made sure no one was home. We'd park our car in the front of the house and knock on the door or ring the doorbell. If someone answered, we'd ask if a made-up person was there and then say "Oh sorry, we must have the wrong house." If no one was home, we'd drive my car around the corner and park in the alley. Then we'd walk down the alley and break in the back door of the house (most people left their doors unlocked back then). We'd quickly look for anything of value that would fit in our pockets.

We didn't do this very often because we didn't find many things of value. There were a couple of times when the homeowners came home while we were inside so we'd run out the back door before they came in the house. We'd run down the alley and hide in the bushes for a short time to make sure we hadn't been seen. We didn't want to get in my car too quickly because we were afraid someone would see us get in and write down my tag number. That was a sure way to get caught. After waiting in the bushes for about ten minutes and feeling sure no one had seen us, we'd walk slowly, get in my car and slowly drive away to not attract any attention.

After trying this for a little while, we decided it was best to just steal auto parts for the wrecking yard. That was sure money. We knew the more times we stole things, the more chances we had of getting caught and our luck would eventually run out. We didn't quit, though, because we had gotten used to having extra money. We slowed down a little and began to be more careful.

Life with Uncle George & Grandma

Well, I made it through the winter and spring and now it was the summer again. Getting to stay with Uncle George and Grandma as a teen turned out to be one of the best times in my life. I was living with my own family that really loved and cared for me. I had a place to come to and not feel like an outsider or a guest. I knew I could just come in the door, sit down and relax, have a good home-cooked meal, and sleep in my own bed. I could talk to Uncle George and Grandma about things I couldn't with other people. They understood me and knew all about where I came from.

The time living with them made me realize that I needed to make some big changes in my life. I give them credit to this day for every good thing that has happened in my life. They were such a good influence on me and believed in me when nobody else did. When I went to live with them this time, I didn't think very highly of myself and thought I would always be in trouble. Seeing my Uncle George being happy with almost no education (he could barely read and write), working hard making minimum wage and yet still being so content really made a positive impression on me. I had lived with different families and some made a very good living and others were well-off, but none of the families seemed to be as content as my Uncle George and my grandparents.

Maybe living on the farm and dealing with nature most of their lives helped Uncle George and my grandparents understand life better than most people. Now when I look back, I realize what an important part of my life they were to me. They are the reason I am alive today and the reason I was able to have success later in life with my work, family, and children.

Gang Life Not So Cool
School in the eleventh grade had started. Frankie and I were running together all the time. I didn't see Rodney much anymore because he was always getting into some kind of trouble with the law. He wasn't cautious enough and got caught stealing, which made me nervous. I had seen him and some other members of our gang get caught and go to jail and I didn't want this to happen to me.

Carl, a friend of mine, who was not in our gang, got caught stealing a car and went to jail for a couple of months while awaiting trial. Frankie and I went to court when his trial came up because we wondered what might happen to us if we got caught stealing. We found out the trial was coming up in a few days and decided to skip school that day. When we walked into the courthouse, everyone was looking at us, I guess since we were so young, they were wondering why we were not in school. We asked around to find out which courtroom was holding Carl's trial. We walked into the courtroom, which was empty except for Carl and his lawyer, the prosecuting lawyer, and four people we assumed to be part of Carl's family. The trial was very short, the judge said he was guilty and gave him two years in the penitentiary.

Frankie and I got out of there in a hurry after we heard the sentence. It made us think about how lucky we were not getting caught for stealing cars for joy rides and other stealing escapades. We had been close to getting caught a few times. This made me not want to steal anymore, even if I was low on money. I did stop stealing for a while.

Runaway Marriage Foiled
Later, during the school year, Frankie and I met a couple of girls and for the rest of the year, we spent most of our time double-dating. We'd go to the drive-in theater and hang out at Holley's drive-in restaurant or at Frankie's girlfriend Loretta's house.
When we weren't hanging out with the girls, we were stealing to make extra money. Christmas was coming and I ended up having a good Christmas that year at Uncle George and Grandma's house, along with

my aunts, uncles and some cousins. Christmas Day evening I went to my girlfriend Carol's house for dinner.

A few days after Christmas, Carol told me thought she was pregnant. We began to talk about getting married. At first, it made me sad to think about getting married at this point in my life. I was disappointed in myself for creating this situation but wanted to do what was right for the baby I was bringing into this world. I cared a lot for Carol but was not ready for marriage. I always thought I would never marry because I wanted to be like my Uncle George. He was over 40 years old and was very happy not being married. I always thought I would do the same.

Carol was fourteen and I was fifteen. We both had jobs after school. I worked for Hinner's Pharmacy and Carol at the T G & Y store, making the same money as me.

We didn't tell any of our friends we had to get married because back then everyone looked down on girls for getting pregnant before marriage. We didn't think her parents would let her get married, so we decided to run away to get married. We decided to try a Justice of the Peace. We heard of other high school students who ran off and got married in one of the small towns south of Oklahoma City, and a few had even gone to Texas. Our plan was to skip school and tell her parents and my grandma we were all dressed up for picture day at school. We picked February 2, 1954, for our "Runaway Marriage!"

The day before our "Big Day", I went to bed early but couldn't stop thinking about getting married. What was my life was going to be like married? I had broken a promise to myself to never marry. I wondered if getting married was going to keep me from having a happy life like my Uncle George. I worried about what Uncle George and Grandma would think about me. Would they be disappointed in me? How was I going to support a wife and new baby? Would I go back to my old habit of stealing?

I thought of how happy Uncle George was making a small amount of money. Something in the back of my mind told me I wouldn't be happy unless I made lots of money. I had spoiled myself with my stealing antics. I had gotten use to having a nice car and plenty of money. These thoughts went over and over in my head all night long.

The next morning I picked up Carol for school as usual. Instead of going to school, we headed south on Highway 77, stopping at every little town and going to the local Justice of the Peace to see if someone would marry us. Everyone said Carol was too young and we needed her parents' written permission. We hit several more towns before giving up and heading back to Oklahoma City to see if Carol's mother would give her permission.

Rent a Place—Get Married

It was a long drive home and we arrived at Carol's house about 4 p.m. We went in and the look on our faces let Carol's mother know something was wrong. I liked Carol's mother and we always got along very good, but this time I couldn't say anything.

Carol and her mother went to the kitchen for a few minutes and when they came out, her mother said, "So you want to marry my daughter?"

And I managed to get a *"yes, ma'am"* out.

She said, "Okay, to do this you have to have a place to live."

She handed me the classified page from a local newspaper with a garage apartment for rent ad circled, and it was located only a few blocks away.

She said, "You two go check this out and I will call the preacher and see if he can come by this evening to marry you."

I don't know why – but we felt we just had to get married that day! Later on, after we realized how easy it was this way, we wished we had tried this way first. The apartment was above a garage with outside stairs going up to it with the owner living in the house in front. The apartment was one big room with a bed in one corner, a little table and two chairs in another corner, and a sofa on the opposite side of the room. The kitchen area was tiny with a few cabinets, a small fridge, and two-burner gas stove. The bathroom was in the back corner. We said we would take it the minute we saw it. We paid the rent of thirty-five dollars for one month and were on our way to getting married!

When we got back to Carol's house, her mother had arranged for the preacher to be there at 7 p.m. We needed someone to witness besides Carol's mother. So I went over to Barry's house and got him and his girlfriend. I was glad everything was happening so fast because if I had time to think, I might have backed out. I was scared to death of getting married!

Mr. Hinner paid me twelve dollars a week and the only other honest job I had ever had was a paper route. The only way I knew to make money was by stealing things. But I knew I could not keep doing this. I decided to quit school and get a full-time job but I knew that might be a problem because of my age.

The wedding was quick since it was just us, Carol's parents, Barry and his girlfriend, and the preacher. Not much happened after the wedding, we just went to our apartment and that was it. That night I tried not to think about how I was going to make a living. The next few days we didn't go to school but I did go by that evening and tell Mr. Hinner at the drugstore that I had gotten married. He told me I could take a few days off and he raised my pay to fifteen dollars per week.

Married Boy Needs an Honest Job

After I married, I went back to school for a short time, but I didn't make enough money to get by and the money I had socked away was getting used up fast.

My shop teacher Mr. Jameson helped me get a job at a trucking company working on their trucks. I only lasted a few months. I got mad at my boss and he fired me. When I started looking for another job, no one would hire me because of my age, so I started back to my old trade of stealing auto parts. I went back and talked to Mr. Jameson to see if he could help me. He told me about a friend's son who was unable to find a job, so he joined the Air Force. I liked that idea because I knew at least we would have food and a place to live. In March of 1955, when I turned 17 years old, I joined the Air Force. By this time we knew Carol was not going to have a baby. At first, I was disappointed because I was excited about starting a family and having a child of my own. I felt like getting married and having a child would make us a real family. I hoped having a real family would make a big difference in how I lived my life. I began to dream of a totally different life, very different than the one I had been living.

Bus Ride to a New Life

I was accepted into the Air Force and was scheduled to board a bus in Oklahoma City. Carol drove me down to the Air Force Induction Center and I had to say my goodbyes.

About 4 hours later, I boarded an Air Force bus headed for Lackland Air Force Base in San Antonio, Texas. As the bus began to pull out of the driveway, I was overcome with emotion. I was sad and relieved at the same time to be starting a new life. I was uncertain about my future but believed God and my guardian angels helped to get me on this bus.

But here is what God ultimately used to turn my life around and get me off the stealing path: My two daughters!

My Daughters: Dianna (born 1961) & Sheryl (born 1960)

Other Pictures of My Life

1945 Age 7

1951 Age 13

1953 Age 15

Grandma, Grandpa & Uncle George (1938)

AFTERWORD

As I look back now, I'm sure my guardian angels were looking over me, joining the Air Force gave me some of the best times of my life. A few years later Carol and I had our first beautiful baby girl (Sheryl) and a year later, we had another beautiful girl (Dianna). I thought life was great from that point forward. I never wanted to go back to stealing or doing anything that would mess up what I had now.

The hardest part of going into the Air Force was being away from my wife Carol during boot camp. The Air Force discovered I had an aptitude for electronics and mechanics. This served me well, as I only had to serve four weeks in boot camp before they sent me to engine and aircraft mechanics school at Sheppard Air Force Base in Wichita Falls, Texas, where I was number one in my class. Carol and I were able to get a little apartment in town and be together again.

Before I left Sheppard Air Force Base, I went AWOL for a month because they were going to send me to Tule, Greenland. I didn't want to go there because it was so cold and I couldn't take my wife along. During the month I was AWOL, my mom, who didn't like me being in the Air Force, managed to get me a mail order ordained minister certificate. She remembered World War II and was afraid there might be another war and thought I might get killed. So I went along with my mother's idea. There was no way was I going to Tule, Greenland! I went back to base with my mail order ordained minister papers, claiming I needed to be released from the military for religious reasons when in truth I wasn't even going to church.

But that didn't fly at all and my superior officers just laughed at me and looked at me like I was an idiot. They kept me for quite a few hours in the commander's office and proceeded to tell me I was going to be reprimanded. I told them I didn't care because I was not going to Tule, Greenland! Again they looked at me like I was a dumb hick and told me that ship had already sailed and another person was sent to Tule in my place. Now I was in big trouble! So instead of leaving Sheppard Air Force Base after six months, I was held there over a year.

After my AWOL stink, I was given grunge duty of digging out sidewalks by the barracks. They put a wimpy First Lieutenant in charge of me who wore a dippy summer uniform and I secretly called him Jungle Jim. I would start digging until he left, then I would go into a nearby barracks and lay on a cot by the window to watch out for him. When I saw him coming, I would run out the back door of the barracks and go back to my digging. He wasn't too bright and only checked on me once a day so it took him quite a while to figure out I wasn't doing much of anything. One day he came at a different time, sneaked in the back of the barracks and caught me. He immediately took me back to the commander's office. They said I was in a lot of trouble but in two weeks they sent me off to Dover Air Force Base in Dover, Delaware. There I worked as an aircraft mechanic on the C-124 Globemaster Aircraft.

While at Dover I spent a few times in the brig for various infractions. Most were minor events where some of us guys and Carol would take a little vacation in Washington D.C. or Wilmington, Delaware. We would drive up there on a weekend if we heard a snow storm was coming and then call into the base saying we couldn't drive back because of the weather. That worked for us a few times until our commanding officer figured it out and threw us in the brig for a few days. One time I just called from my home in Delaware and said I couldn't drive to work because of the snow and my commanding officer sent some guys in a big all-terrain vehicle with tires as tall as a man to pick me up and make sure I came to work on the base that day!

When I first arrived at Dover, another airman who had rank on me was harassing and bullying me, calling me stupid and other names. I put up with him for over a week. Then one day we were all sitting and riding on a trailer to another area on base when he sits down beside me and started talking trash to me. He was a big man, where I was small-framed and only 5'8" tall. Some people have even accused me of having *little man syndrome*, which may be true since I had suffered abuse from my step-father and big guys at school attacking me. Anyway, something snapped in me. I jumped up and started kicking my trash talker with my steel-toed boots and he fell off the heavy-duty trailer filled with men. The trailer ran him and broke both of his legs.
I became a hero with the crew for standing up to him, as he had bullied all the airmen in my crew.

However, I got in trouble for hurting him and got two weeks in the brig. I went through a court on base where I had stripes taken away. The brig wasn't' all that bad, as they would let me walk down to the commissary to buy magazines and snacks. Also, every few days they let me go off base to see my wife, Carol. Our crew never knew what happened to the bully because we never saw him again. After a few months, I decided to get a second job because we just didn't have enough money to rent a decent place to live. My regular duty on base was midnight until seven in the morning. I got a second job working at a garage in town as a mechanic working from 8 AM to 3 p.m. and on days off from the base I would work eight to five. I only slept about four hours a day.

I never slept a lot during my life until after I had my heart attack at age fifty-seven. A few Sergeants who really liked me would have me over to their house for dinner. My whole life, people either really liked me or hated me…not many in-between relationships. The best thing about being in Dover was I made good money between the Air Force and my other job. I was able to buy us a place to live and brand new 1960 Mercury. I bought it and surprised my wife when I picked her up from the hospital with our first child Sheryl.

Another great thing about my life at Dover was my Air Force buddies I made while stationed there. We had a lot of fun together, such as going to Rehoboth Beach or attending an Air Force buddy's Polish three-day wedding and celebration in Wilmington. Some of us Air Force buddies are still in touch today. Over the years we have had reunions in places like Chicago, Nashville, Memphis, Dayton, and Granbury, Texas.

Toward the end of my enlistment of four years in the Air Force, I was told to pack some clothes for a week or two for a TDY trip (temporary duty). I didn't think much of it, since I had been on other TDY trips to no less than Tule, Greenland, for a month, the Philippines for a few weeks, and to Ft. Polk, Louisiana, a few times. However, on this trip, we went to Chateauroux, France, for two weeks. We flew out thinking we were going to Berlin but we were rerouted to Africa to a Belgian Congo air base in Leopoldville. It was a special assignment for the United Nation Operation in the Congo. We were not allowed to wear our uniforms or go into town. I was in the Congo close to a year.

When I left on this supposedly short TDY trip, Carol was pregnant with our second child. There was no phone or mail communication service available after arriving in Leopoldville. Luckily I was able to contact Carol while in France and told her we might be gone for six months. She decided to go stay with her mother in El Paso, Texas until I returned. I didn't even know when my second child was born or if I had a boy or girl until I got out of Africa. When I got back to Dover, my new daughter Dianna was eight months old.

I was kept an additional six months at Dover before I was released. Maybe the Air Force was paying me back for my AWOL antics or maybe my guardian angels were trying to teach me a lesson. So my four years turned into almost six years. Funny how I was so happy when I got out of the Air Force, but when I look back now, I know my years there saved my life. I think the structure and the security helped me to grow up and it was the best thing that ever happened to me. The Air Force helped me to make different kinds of friends, view life differently, and develop self-confidence. My guardian angels knew I couldn't change my life without getting away from my bad environment in Oklahoma City.

After I finished my tour in the Air Force, we moved back to Oklahoma City, where I tried working at various jobs for other people. But I didn't take orders well, so I went into business for myself. My first business was a recreation center open until midnight, with pool tables and slot cars, and where we only served soft drinks. It mostly interested young people in their early twenties. But it was a short-lived fad and my overhead was more than my revenue, so I had to close down after one year.

My next business was a carpet store catering to residential customers, but it didn't do well either due to mismanagement of funds and my lack of experience at running my own business. I had personal financial problems at that time, too, because my house in Oklahoma City had a major fire due to my car catching on fire in the garage. While I was waiting on the insurance to pay, I took money from my business to fix up the house. However, the insurance stiffed me, as their home office was out of state and they never paid up on my claim. I had to file for bankruptcy and was devastated. So I packed up my family, loaded our belongings on a U-Haul truck and moved to Dallas, Texas.

I got a job working nights doing electrical inspection work at Ling-Temco-Vought on the LTV A-7E Corsair II fighter planes and started my own carpet laying business during the daytime hours. I worked hard day and night, only sleeping four to five hours at a time and after a couple of years, it paid off. I also opened up a Kawasaki motorcycle dealership and at one time had two dealerships, along with my floor contracting business and also a commercial construction business. I experienced the financial success I had always dreamed of and it was legal, too.

My floor covering contracting business grew fast. I had carpeting jobs for apartments, government buildings such as the federal building in downtown Dallas, and commercial carpeting for many businesses in the Dallas/Ft. Worth area.

However, after all this hard work and success my twenty-five years of marriage fell apart. Maybe it was because I was working too many hours away from home or because my wife Carol had too much money and time on her hands. I really don't know for sure why we both grew so far apart. We split up a year after building our dream house – a unique round house in a prestigious neighborhood, which I partially built as an attempt to save our failing marriage.

We were separated for five years. I stayed separated for as long as I did, hoping Carol and I could work things out. She finally filed for divorce and I did not contest it or anything she asked for, as I thought I could be financially successful again. But that did not happen. I lost my drive for money and success and would never regain it.

After our split, I went through a long depression. I had falsely thought money and success would guarantee me personal happiness. I learned then the true meaning of the old saying, "Money can't buy happiness."

I took a regular job working for ITT Finance Company calling on dealerships and checking their floor planning. I made a good living wage and managed to hide my depression over the failure of my marriage by keeping busy and *drinking a lot.*

I never liked to be alone. I would be the first one to go to any office party or have drinks with the guys after work. At one time I realized I was having to take a drink at 9 a.m. in the morning if I had a sales meeting at 10 or 11 a.m., so I decided right then I was not going to let alcohol rule my life.

Then one day after many dates and romances that I just could not commit to, I went to a church singles Christmas party. It was in the home of an older couple who taught a church singles class for the First Baptist Church in McKinney, Texas. I just had mouth surgery and really did not feel like going, but at the last minute changed my mind. A gal I was casually dating had invited me. Well, I showed up but she was not there yet. Funny thing is, I had never attended that church or singles class or knew anyone at the party. I was just there to meet my casual girlfriend. However, this was before cell phones and I hadn't bothered to call her and tell her I was coming after all.

As I was waiting for her to arrive, I noticed a pretty lady with two children. I enjoyed watching her try to corral her two children ages nine and twelve. They weren't bad kids, just full of energy and fun-loving. She came over and visited with me for a while and then they all starting playing Trivial Pursuit. Oh my goodness, I hated such games because you had to have done well in school to play that game. The lady was enjoying the game and ignoring me, so I decided to leave since my friend hadn't shown up. In fact, I never heard from my friend again, and when I tried to call, her number was not even a working number anymore. This made me think even more my guardian angels were just trying to get me to the party to meet Judy.

As I was going out the door, she came over to me and gave me her real estate card and asked me to call her sometime if I was ever interested in buying some real estate.

Over the next few days, I kept thinking about the lady named Judy. I carried on a fight within myself. She had children! First of all, I had told myself I would never fall for anyone with children, plus never marry again as it had been over ten years since I had been with my first wife. I could tell she was the type of woman that was not into casual relationships.

In spite of myself, I found myself calling her asking to look at some income property, a house I could rent out. I was not really going to buy anything but wanted to check her out some more.

The party where I met Judy was on December 10, 1984, and we married on June 19, 1985. Since then we built two houses, moved many times, tackled new jobs, raised her two children, and were full-timers in a motor home for over ten years.

Along the way, Judy finished her education and got a masters degree in library science, while I acquired some great jobs and some bad ones. Shortly after Judy finished her education degree and started teaching I had a heart attack and triple by-pass surgery. My health has been quite a challenge for the last 20 years.

Judy and I have enjoyed over thirty-two years together since our guardian angels got us together. A day doesn't go by that I don't thank God for getting me this far in life!

Judy and I have managed to blend our two families together. We have four wonderful grown children, three son-in-laws, and a daughter-in-law, not to mention thirteen grandchildren and nine great-grandchildren. I also have a grown foster son, Willie, whom I hope I have helped in some small way like Mr. Jameson did for me.

My life has come a long way from a hole in the side of a mountain in Arizona. Thanks to my guardian angels and God's Grace, I can say, "Life is good!"

Made in the USA
Coppell, TX
07 March 2024